"A remarkable story of a fallen cycling hero." —CYCLINGREVIEW.NL

"Brutally honest." —*CYCLINGNEWS*

"Arguably the most shocking yet. . . . It is the uncomfortably raw, matter-of-fact descriptions of the hedonistic lifestyle of a professional cyclist just one decade ago, and the depths to which he sank as he tried to navigate his way through that minefield, which are most shocking." —*THE TELEGRAPH*

"A staggering underworld of blood bags, testosterone patches, and injections. No one is spared." —ERIC PALMEN, *BIOGRAFIEPORTAAL*

"Unlike others—David Millar, Tyler Hamilton—Dekker doesn't try to pass responsibility for his doping elsewhere: it was his choice. He shows a self-awareness that's been lacking in most recent 'chamoirs' and has been absent from most doping kiss-and-tells. Dekker's willingness to accept responsibility for his own actions is refreshing." —*PODIUM CAFÉ*

"The most shocking doping memoir professional cycling has produced." —DANIEL FRIEBE, AUTHOR OF *EDDY MERCKX: THE CANNIBAL*

"*Descent* . . . has something that one rarely comes across in a cycling memoir—vulnerability." —ERIK RASCHKE, *CYCLINGTIPS*

"It's been a long time since there was so much ado about a cycling book. It's a shock when you realize that a cyclist has a rock-n-roll life instead of a monk's existence. It's time to read it yourself and judge it."

"*Descent* should also be course material for cycling: Every commissaire, every DCO, every DS, every wrench monkey, everybody should be made to read *Descent*, not to see where Dekker failed himself but to see where the sport failed him and to learn how not to let it fail others."

"Thomas Dekker has done something brave here: He has opened sutured wounds with the hope that the rot will dry up. And for that alone we should be thankful."

"What a relief it is to hear a former pro sportsman take responsibility for his actions. Perhaps this is what makes *Descent* so different; it certainly accounts for it being unputdownable."

"For the average cycling lover, this is a hard confrontation with 'dirty' cycling."

"Readers will be shocked by many passages about sex, drugs, prostitutes, and the hedonistic excessiveness and egotistical drive that it takes to succeed in pro cycling. . . . Each chapter is a conscious move toward the final stage of self-destruction, and when the end arrives, the reader, too, feels ruined."

DESCENT

MY EPIC FALL FROM
CYCLING SUPERSTARDOM
TO DOPING DEAD END

DESCENT

THOMAS DEKKER
AS TOLD TO THIJS ZONNEVELD

TRANSLATED FROM THE DUTCH BY DAVID DOHERTY

Boulder, Colorado

Copyright © 2017 by Thomas Dekker and Thijs Zonneveld.
Published by agreement with Overamstel Uitgevers B.V.
English translation copyright © 2017 by David Doherty.
First Dutch edition published by Overamstel Uitgevers B.V. in 2016.
First UK edition published by Ebury Press in 2017.
US edition edited by Ted Costantino.

3002 Sterling Circle, Suite 100
Boulder, CO 80301–2338 USA

VeloPress is the leading publisher of books on endurance sports. Focused on cycling, triathlon, running, swimming, and nutrition/diet, VeloPress books help athletes achieve their goals of going faster and farther. Preview books and contact us at velopress.com.

Distributed in the United States and Canada by Ingram Publisher Services

A Cataloging-in-Publication record for this book is available from the Library of Congress.
ISBN 9781937715809

This paper meets the requirements of ANSI/NISO Z39.48-1992 (Permanence of Paper).

Art Direction by Vicki Hopewell
Cover design by theBookDesigners
Cover photograph by Franck Fife/Getty Images
Text set in Heroic Condensed, Trade Gothic, and Freight Text

17 18 19 / 10 9 8 7 6 5 4 3 2 1

CONTENTS

1
IN THE HOTEL

IT'S A THOUSAND SHADES OF DARK. The curtains are drawn, the door is locked. The only light is the dim glow of the bedside lamp. Shadows creep across the carpet and up the wall. The picture hanging there is the kind you find in countless hotel rooms—an anonymous print of some flower.

I'm lying on the bed in my jogging pants and T-shirt. I haven't even bothered to take off my shoes. A thick needle is sticking out of my arm, attached to a drip. My blood runs dark red through the plastic tube. Slowly it fills the bag that's sitting on a digital scale on the floor.

In the corner of the room, far from the light, a man is sitting in a chair. His foot bobs up and down as he jots something in his diary. Every few minutes he glances at the scale. I met him for the first time half an hour ago in the hotel lobby. He introduced himself as Dr. Fuentes. Beige trousers, checked shirt, and a face that is instantly forgotten. He smells of cigarette smoke. We have barely spoken a word to each other. His English is basic and my Spanish nonexistent.

I don't think he even knows who I am. Not that it matters.

I haven't come here to talk.

I stare at the blood in the bag. It's as if it isn't mine. As if it isn't even real. I thought it would be different, the first time, that I would be excited, nervous—like a kid stealing candy from the corner shop. But there is no thrill, no jangling nerves. This is a simple transaction. Doping is business. It just happens to be one you need to hide from as many people as possible.

Fifteen minutes go by, and Dr. Fuentes gets out of his chair. He removes the needle from my arm and wipes away the blood with a cotton ball. He holds out a Sharpie and says in a thick Spanish accent, "I give you number. Twenty-four. Two four. You must write here." He points to the bag of blood. I sit up, take the marker, and write the number on the bag. He nods and says, "We are done."

I pull my tracksuit top over my T-shirt and shake his hand. He opens the door and mumbles something indecipherable. I step into the hallway—the light is so bright it hurts my eyes.

The door clicks shut behind me.

There's no way back from here.

2
DEAD ORDINARY

I GREW UP IN AN ORDINARY FAMILY in an ordinary house on an ordinary street in a small town by the name of Dirkshorn. It's slap-bang in the middle of the pan-flat landscape of northern Holland, little more than a dot on the map: 12 streets, a church, a supermarket, a football club, and a fish-and-chip takeout. A carnival comes to Dirkshorn once a year. That aside, nothing ever happens.

My parents are ordinary too. Bart and Marja. Salt of the earth, you might say. Mom works as a swimming pool attendant in the next town. Dad is a baggage handler at Schiphol Airport. Five mornings a week for 30 years he's been getting up at 4:30 to head for Amsterdam, lunch box crammed with sandwiches, to lug other people's suitcases from one place to another. Dinner is on the table at 5:30 every evening; Dad does the cooking. Standard Dutch fare for the most part: cauliflower, meat, and potatoes. On Sundays we'd always get something from Joep's takeout. My folks earn enough to make ends meet, and they take good care of what they own. I spent my whole childhood whizzing around on secondhand roller skates. They were good enough.

I have a loving mother. The kind who has orange juice and biscuits waiting for you when you come home from school. In her whole life she has only been really angry with me once, when I was very little. I can't even remember what I'd done to upset her.

My father is a typical northerner. The strong, silent type—verging on gruff, even—but he has a big heart and wears it firmly on his sleeve. He's not afraid to speak his mind, but he seldom has to; what he's thinking is written on his face. More often than not he's in good spirits, but when his lip starts to tremble, you know there's a storm brewing. His face is sometimes etched with lines, a sign that he's worried and no stranger to worrying. It wouldn't surprise me if most of his worries have been about me. I think at times he wishes he could still hold on to me the way he used to when we'd cycle over to see Grandma when I was a kid: one hand resting on the back of my neck to stop me falling and keep me on the straight and narrow.

My sister is named Floortje. She's two years younger than me. We have always got along well. We were playmates all through childhood and happily spent entire days in each other's company. On weekends, when Mom and Dad were sleeping in, we'd creep downstairs in the cold, dark house and snuggle up under a blanket on the couch to watch cartoons.

As a boy I was always outdoors. When I wasn't knocking a ball around on the empty lot around the corner or over by the noise barrier along the main road, you could find me playing soldiers or swimming in a lake or the outdoor pool along the way. I was a member of the tennis club, the football club, the skating club. Lack of talent didn't stop me being fanatical about all three. I played for FC Dirkshorn and made my way through the junior ranks from the Fs to the Ds. Granddad used to come and watch me play every week, and he'd give me a guilder if I scored. Sometimes I was so eager to impress him I would charge right through the defender. If we lost, I was in a foul mood. It was the same with every sport. I could fly into a rage if things didn't go my way. All the same, I knew better than to throw a tantrum. If I had hurled my racket to the ground when I lost at tennis, Dad would have marched onto the court and dragged me off by the hair.

I went to school in Dirkshorn. There were only eight children in my class all the way through junior high. Our favorite playground game was marbles. I was determined to have more than anyone else. Sometimes I sold my marbles to the other kids—and then proceeded to win them back again. I must have earned hundreds of guilders that way. I saved it all up for later, to fulfill my dream of buying a flashy car. I have no idea where it comes from, my love of material things. Not from my parents, that's for sure. My sister has no appetite for bling either.

Our summer vacations were much like everyone else's. Mom and Dad in the front seat of the car, Floortje and me in the back with currant buns, Fruittella, and comic books to keep us quiet. Most years we went camping in France, to campsites with a swimming pool, a ping-pong table, and those toilets you had to squat over. It was either that or Center Parcs or Gran Dorado: a couple of weeks in a holiday bungalow that was exactly the same as the one next to it and the one next to that and the hundreds of others that filled the park.

One thing's for sure: I was never one of those troubled kids who are destined to go off the rails from an early age. Our parents showered us with love. Our house wasn't a place of fighting or endless arguments. If anything, we were the opposite of a problem family.

My boyhood can be summed up in a single word: ordinary.

Make that two: dead ordinary.

3

LOVE AT FIRST SIGHT

IT WAS MY BIRTHDAY PRESENT when I turned 11: my first racing bike. So beautiful I could have wept. Black with white accents—the colors of the Dutch professional PDM team back in the day—and "Concorde" emblazoned on the down tube. The frame was bought to grow into, saddle as low as it could go. To negotiate my way through the 12 gears, I had to fiddle with controls mounted on the frame. The pedals had straps that you pulled tight around your feet. A pair of cycling shoes was thrown in for good measure, black with plastic soles.

My first meters on my very own racing bike were from the living room to the utility room off the kitchen. Easy does it, skirting the dining table and wobbling past the TV, a narrow escape for the vase of flowers I passed along the way. Dad grinning from ear to ear, Mom looking a little worried.

Dad had bought my pride and joy at Hans Langerijs, the bike shop in the nearby town of Schagen. A racing bike meant I could join the summer training sessions organized by the skating club where I did my circuits of the rink in winter. I was no great shakes at skating, never really got the hang of the technique. I didn't have the power either. I was small and skinny, legs like lollipop sticks. The bigger kids shot past me on the ice as if I wasn't even there and left me plugging away in their wake. But giving up wasn't an option. It never even occurred to me. All the kids in the north of Holland spent the winter skating, so I did too.

Cycling came more naturally than skating. I started to cover longer distances with Dad: 30 or 35 kilometers out toward the dunes, along the coast and the Hondsbossche seawall, battling into the wind all the way there and then being blown back home. On Friday evenings, Dad would join us on a group ride with the skating club, 90 minutes at most. Just a bunch of boys and girls from the neighborhood.

But cycling was a magnet, and I was a paper clip. It tugged at me. The sheen of the bikes as they sped past when I went to see a criterium race with Dad, the smell of the massage oil. This was different from skating or football. It was more heroic, guts and glory. I looked on breathless as these grown men pushed themselves to the limit, biting back the pain, snot hanging off their chins. Compared with cycling, other sports were child's play.

I was gripped by the epic man-to-man battles I saw on TV. I remember the 1996 Tour de France, when Miguel Indurain bit the dust. He was my hero. I wanted him to win more than anything, and I felt sure he would triumph over Bjarne Riis. It wasn't to be. Indurain cracked on the flanks of the Port de Larrau, a stage that ended in Pamplona—his birthplace. I sat there glued to the screen, shaking my head in disbelief. I just couldn't understand. It was as if he had suddenly become a different rider, too big for his bike and with a grimace on his face that I had never seen before. He seemed to have aged from one day to the next. I remember him being asked to comment that evening back at his hotel, people and cameras everywhere. His words betrayed doubt, his eyes despair. "I don't know what the future holds," he said, "but I will never be better than I was before." It sounded like a farewell.

I began to ride my own races. Frenetic, one-off races in the very north of Holland, in villages with names like Wervershoof and Hippolytushoef. They usually coincided with the annual fair. I raced lap after lap, competing against local kids my age, red in the face, going hell for leather. It usually ended in a sprint, not my strongest suit. I even lost to girls, many of whom were much stronger than me at that age. It pissed me off no end.

My dad bought clip-in pedals for my racing bike. They were purple, made by Look. I went for a quick spin in the neighborhood to try them out before my next training ride. Dad had warned me to be careful not to keel over when I stopped. I shrugged off his words only to end up flat on my back at the first crossroads, unable to get my shoes out of the pedals. A man came over to ask if I was okay. "Yeah, sure," I stammered. I was more worried about my clothes than anything. The fall left me with a hole in my cycling shorts. "Can I get a new pair?" I asked Mom as soon as I got home. "No," she said, shaking her head. "The padding still looks fine to me."

Cycling was taking up more and more of my time. Two rides a week became three, became four. Dad and I began to cover longer distances, striking out for destinations farther afield.

In the summer of 1998 we were on vacation at a French campsite. In the mornings we'd go for a ride, and in the afternoons we'd watch the Tour de France on a little TV in the campsite cafeteria. Dad with a beer, me with a soda. Dutch cycling wasn't worth shit in those days, but in 1998 all that changed: it was the Tour when Michael Boogerd went like a rocket. In his red, white, and blue Dutch road champion jersey he was giving the best riders in the world a run for their money on the climbs. It was the spark that lit the flame in a 14-year-old cycling fanatic. I yelled at the TV, urging him on, hoping with everything I had in me that he would hang in there and not be dropped by the other contenders. At night, I would lie on my blow-up mattress staring up at the roof of the tent, dreaming of myself in the Tour. The victories. The jerseys. Taking the lead as a group of rivals died a thousand deaths trying to hold my wheel.

When we got back home, I came across a poster of Michael Boogerd in a magazine. In no time, it was hanging on my bedroom wall.

That was when I knew for certain. I was going to be a cyclist too.

4
FIRST CALL

IN THE SHOWERS, I LOOKED AROUND at the guys I had just competed against. It was one of my first official races. They were yelling, joking around, telling tall tales from the race. Some of them were useless, some I looked up to. Often they were the bigger kids, the ones with their adolescent growth spurt behind them. A few of them even had pubes. I looked down at my own tackle. Not a hair to be seen. Not even a light dusting.

My performance in those early races was nothing to write home about. Weighing in at a mere 99 pounds, I was blown away in the frantic charge for the finish line. Back then, almost every race was won by Wim Stroetinga—he sprinted like he'd been shot from a revolver. On the track, Niki Terpstra was already making a name for himself. He was a bit chubby, but he rode at a killer pace.

Every weekend there was another race to enter. We traveled the length and breadth of the country: Dad, Mom, Floortje, and me. It was like moving house every time we set off: the back seat piled high with cycling gear, sandwiches, and currant buns, and in the trunk an ice chest packed with cans of Fristi and Coke nestled alongside my new racing bike—a blue Simon, made in Zaandam. To make sure everything would fit, Dad splurged on a Volkswagen camper van. A wise move, especially when Floortje was bitten by the cycling bug too. She didn't stick with it long, but there was no doubting her talent. She even finished second in a national junior time trial championship, ahead of future world and Olympic champion Marianne Vos. It must have been tough for her that family life revolved around me so much of the time, but she never once complained. At least, not that I heard.

Slowly but surely I began to improve. In the Tour de Achterveld, a kind of weeklong stage race for young boys and girls, I finished second. My parents weren't able to come and watch every day, so I stayed with a host family. It was the first time I had ever been away from home alone. I was so nervous that I hardly slept a wink all night. Not because I was lonely but because this was starting to feel like the real thing, complete with time trials, pretty girls, juries, and barriers to keep the spectators at bay.

I sailed through the youth categories, and with each passing year my ambition grew and my dreams became bigger and brighter. My parents encouraged me but never pushed. Dad was fanatical, but he never stood on the sidelines screaming his head off, and he was never disappointed if I wasn't up there with the leaders. As long as I did my best, that was what mattered to him. To me that was only logical: I always did my best. Those were the days! To Mom it was all the same whether I came 1st, 2nd, or 356th: she would have been just as happy to see me playing tennis or hanging around the school playground with my friends.

In all that time I only saw Dad angry once. It was after the Omloop van de Maasvallei, a race for novices in the province of Limburg, 300 kilometers south of Dirkshorn. Dad drove me down there the day before, and we stayed at a little bed-and-breakfast in the riverside town of Elsloo. I was convinced it was a course made for me, if only because it was among the hills of Limburg and I cherished the secret hope that I was a good climber. Fat chance— I was left for dead before the climbing even began. The weather was on the wet side, and not long after the start a slick stretch of cobbles led down from Maasberg. I was scared shitless and made the descent with my brakes squeezed as tight as my ass cheeks. The peloton sped off ahead of me before we were 8 kilometers in. I didn't see them again for the rest of the day. I turned and rode back to the start alone, where Dad was still standing around chatting with other parents. He saw me, and the words "F'ckn' 'ell" came out through clenched teeth.

The drive back to Dirkshorn lasted a lifetime. We sat there in almost total silence, my dad and I. Was I more pissed off or ashamed? It was a toss-up. Dad couldn't understand it. It wasn't because I had been dropped by the pack—shit happens. What he couldn't stomach was the fact that I had caved in before the race had even properly begun. When we were halfway home, somewhere near Utrecht, he said to me, "Well, son, if you slam on the brakes on a downhill run . . ." Then he ruffled my hair and mumbled that next time was sure to be better.

At the end of my first year with the novices, when I was 15, a letter landed on the doormat. The Rabobank logo on the envelope was enough to get my pulse racing. It was an invitation to take part in the Rabo Ardennen Proef—a mini–training camp organized to give the team a closer look at the talented young riders on the circuit. The aim was to handpick the best early on with a view to propelling them to the elite level in three stages: through the juniors (Under-18s) to the Under-23s and on to the pro circuit. I could hardly believe it—an invitation from Rabobank addressed to me!

When I left for the hotel in the Belgian resort of Spa a few weeks later, I was on cloud nine. Dad drove me to the pickup station in De Meern, and from there a bus took us to the Ardennes, with a few more stops along the way. The selection included a slew of good riders from my generation: Marc de Maar, Reinier Honig, and Jos Harms to name but three. We were welcomed to the camp by Jan Raas himself, world-class road racer turned team director. We were given Rabobank water bottles for our bikes. Support staff were on hand to attend to our every need, and we trained under the watchful eye of another Dutch cycling hero, Adrie van der Poel. It was unbelievable. In my eyes, Rabobank was as good as it got. The absolute pinnacle.

5
JUNIOR CAMP

ALL THIS TIME I WAS STILL AT SCHOOL. Learning nothing. It was like serving out a jail sentence. I acted the clown, eyed up the girls, and pretty much ignored everything my teachers had to say. I only opened my books when there was a grade at stake. I got away with it for a while, scraping through the first and second years of high school in the top stream and somehow even making it to third year at the same level. But as my interest in cycling soared, my schoolwork took a nosedive.

I had one dream, and that was to become a professional cyclist. Everything that stood in the way was swept aside. Cycling ruled my day from the moment I got up in the morning till my head hit the pillow at night. Through the cycling association I was assigned a coach, René Kos. He drew up training schedules for me, but I always did more than he asked. Toward the end of 2000, shortly before my transition from novice to junior, Dad bought a motor scooter so I could train behind him. When he came home from work in the afternoon, we would ride for hours through the low-lying polders of northern Holland. Every Thursday evening, rain or shine, I rode over to Alkmaar for a training session at the bike track and returned late with my lights shining through the dark. Twenty kilometers there and 20 back.

On weekends, I worked to earn the money to buy new equipment. My parents supported me to the hilt, but I chipped in a fair amount from my own savings. I was determined to buy a Campagnolo Record group for my bike, with carbon brake levers. I had spent months with my nose pressed up against the bike shop window; they cost a whopping 1,600 guilders. I peeled flower bulbs and worked part-time serving coffee at the local furniture showroom. I even did farmwork. With all this and training too, things were pretty busy. Too busy sometimes. I remember coming home in tears one day after getting up at the crack of dawn to work in a greenhouse. "Mom, Dad, I'm so tired. If I have to keep this up I'll never make it as a pro rider."

In the end, I joined the junior ranks riding a bike with a Campagnolo Record group. Paid for with my own hard-earned cash. The carbon wheels to go with it came courtesy of my first sponsorship deal—with my Uncle Claus. The new parts made one hell of a difference. But better still, I began to grow . . . and how! I stretched a good four inches in next to no time. The result was a massive boost to my performance; I was much stronger than I had been in years gone by. I flew through my next races, taking third in the first classic of the season, a result that led national coach Egon van Kessel to select me to ride for my country. I was allowed to take part in races outside Holland, World Cup races for juniors. My first international outing was to Poland—the Coupe du Grudziadz. I had no idea where we were, the food was so shitty we sat there gagging at the table—but I loved every minute of it.

A few months later I was selected for a World Cup race in Austria as a guest rider for the Rabobank junior team. The whole team slept in the same dorm at a boarding school. Johnny Hoogerland was my teammate that week, and it was the race when I first laid eyes on the Italian armada: Vincenzo Nibali, Giovanni Visconti, and Mauro Santambrogio. They all sported identical tracksuits, identical bum bags, identical phones and strutted around like they were cocks of the walk. I was deeply impressed. I've always admired Italy's cycling tradition. There's none of that po-faced Calvinist "let's not get carried away with ourselves" attitude you often see in Holland. I'd much rather see cyclists walk with their shoulders back and their heads held high. In Holland a top athlete is frowned on for driving a Ferrari; in Italy everyone wonders why the hell you'd want to drive anything else.

In the autumn of 2001, I signed with Rabobank. Of course I signed with Rabobank. They wanted me on their junior team, and I would have crawled on my hands and knees to get in if that's what it took. Not only that, but I was selected for my first world championships, in Lisbon.

The juniors were put up in the same hotel as the pros. I met Michael Boogerd and Erik Dekker. They said hello and asked me how I was doing. I don't recall saying much in reply. Not that it mattered. The mere fact that a kid like me was standing there talking to riders I had only ever seen on TV was a thrill in itself. The poster on my bedroom wall had come to life.

Lisbon was also my first encounter with Gerrie Knetemann. He was the national coach for the pros, but he rode behind me in the team car when I did the time trial. He took me aside beforehand, and we spoke for quite a while. He told me he could see that I had what it took, and not just because we hailed from the same part of the country. "Thomas," he said, "you're the complete package. You're a climber, a time trialist, and I can see that you're willing to give it your all. We haven't heard the last of you, boy." I was walking on air. That day I barely had to make an effort on the bike. I had the wind at my back no matter what direction I was cycling in.

Every junior rider at the time was in love with Pleuni Möhlmann, who came away from Lisbon with a silver medal. But I was the one kissing her at the closing party. We fooled around for a while after the championships but never really got it together. Back home the opposite sex was becoming more of a focus too. I started hanging around the little huddles of girls that formed during school break times and noticed that they didn't seem to mind. I understood what they wanted. I gave them attention and time. Both were in plentiful supply; once my training sessions were over, I had nothing else to do. I called girls, e-mailed them, texted them.

I took them out for a bite to eat or to see a film. I never had a steady girlfriend; I tended to get bored after a while. There was always someone sweeter to catch my eye. But if you'd told me at the time that I'd end up sleeping with hundreds of women, I'd have said you were out of your mind.

At school I was on a road to nowhere. I had already been moved down a level and went on to fail my fourth-year exams. And when I joined the Rabobank juniors the following year, things went from bad to worse. I skipped classes so I could train, turned up without my books, and when it came to tests I wrote down the first thing that popped into my head. When my sister handed in my books at the end of the year—I was too busy training to do it myself— they were still wrapped in cellophane. I hadn't opened them once. School was useless, a waste of time, a black hole that swallowed up the precious hours of my life. If Italian had been on the curriculum, I might have sat up and paid attention—that would have been some use to me as a cycling pro. Anything else I dismissed out of hand.

Riding for the Rabobank junior team in 2002, I just kept getting faster. It was such a professional outfit. We were surrounded by coaches, mechanics, and support staff. A training camp was set up for us. The equipment was always up to scratch, and I was riding with the best Dutch juniors of the day, among them Marc de Maar and Tom Veelers. But I was the biggest talent of all. There was no stopping me. I won, won again, and I kept on winning. It sometimes seemed like losing wasn't in my repertoire. I didn't just beat my rivals, I pulverized them. Of the 60 races I rode that year, I won 22 and made the podium 40 times. I was light-years ahead of everyone in the world junior rankings. My confidence grew with every victory. I began to realize that I was more than just another promising rider. My ambitions got bigger, and so did my mouth. I expected the world to revolve around me. I wanted to be the center of attention.

We were out training with the Dutch national selection for the world championships in Zolder when I failed to spot a post. I collided with it at full speed and went flying head over heels. I felt my teeth crunch; in the few seconds before I spat them out, I could feel them rattling around my mouth like marbles in an empty washing machine. I continued my training ride, rode on for hours minus seven teeth. I was unable to eat anything else on the bike. Sitting in the dentist's chair that evening, hunger was gnawing away at my insides.

That crash meant I only ended fourth in the world championship time trial. I can still see myself riding in the road race on the wheel of the last rider; I had a jacket over my jersey. A camera motorbike rode alongside me all the way. The race was broadcast live and I was the talk of the show, but you've seldom seen such a miserable loser in close-up. I'd had it with the whole fucking circus: the tumble I had taken in training, the flat course with no opportunity to make a difference, the final sprint that amounted to little more than a free-for-all. I was pissed off with a vengeance. I expected more. The world of cycling expected more. I wasn't just any old talent. I was Thomas fucking Dekker.

6
THE COMMITMENT

I PICKED UP THE PHONE. "Thomas, it's me." Mom's voice was trembling, furious. The school had just called her; there was no place to hide. She knew I had kept quiet about my grades. She knew I had tossed every letter the school had sent. She knew I had failed my final exams. More than that—she knew I'd had the chance to retake them and hadn't bothered to turn up. I'd been in Spain at the time. Having made the transition from Rabobank's junior team to its Under-23 squad, I had decided that the Tour of Lleida was more important than my exams. Before I left, my parents didn't even know that there were any do-overs—I had fobbed them off with a story about the exam results being delayed. Mom ordered me to come back home immediately. I refused. From Lleida, I traveled through France with the Under-23 team to compete in the Boucles de la Mayenne. Only then did I return to Dirkshorn.

My parents were waiting for me when I got back. I'd never seen them so angry. They felt betrayed. I understood that. They felt deceived. I understood that too. They told me I'd thrown away my future by not turning up for my exams. I nodded. Again, I understood. But as for their plan to send me to college in Den Helder to obtain qualifications in math and economics—no way. Whatever they said, however much they raised their voices, however sweetly they pleaded: point-blank refusal. I had only one answer for them: "I'm never going back to school. I'm going to be a professional cyclist."

This did not go down well. There was only one moment of respite during that week in June, when Dad and I headed out for a training ride around Lake IJssel with the scooter—a trip of 275 kilometers. We stopped for a break halfway. Dad wolfed down a portion of battered fish, I chomped on a Snickers. Then we rode on, never sinking below 30 miles per hour.

That circuit of Lake IJssel was my last long training session before the 2003 Dutch National Championships for Under-23s. It was to be held in Rotterdam, and there was only one climb, a bridge. It wasn't a course that suited me, and it had been agreed beforehand that I would play second fiddle to Hans Dekkers, our team sprinter. But when I went to the front with 3 kilometers to go, my teammates were unable to stay with me. I looked over my shoulder, saw daylight between me and the rest, and shifted up a gear. No one could touch me.

I came home that evening to find the street festooned with flags. Half of Dirkshorn had turned out to welcome me. It was a heartfelt celebration, and many a beer was downed. Late that evening I sat on the couch, face-to-face with my parents. Dad spoke first. "If you don't want to go back to school and you're determined to give cycling the full 100 percent, then so be it." Mom nodded and resigned herself to the inevitable.

For my parents the finest part of my career was already over. From that moment on, I pretty much struck out on my own. I knew what I wanted, and I wasn't about to let anyone come between me and my bike. I began throwing my weight around, playing the cocky bastard. I can still picture myself late one winter evening lining up to get into Jimmy Woo, an Amsterdam nightclub. I was out on the town with a few mates; none of us could have been much older than 20. After an hour of freezing our asses off, we finally made it to the front of the line only to find that the doorman wasn't having it. This wasn't the kind of club to welcome a bunch of young guys from the provinces who were already tanked up on beer. I was furious. I ranted and raved, read him the riot act: "Do you know who I am? Do you know who you're talking to? I'm Thomas Dekker!" My name meant nothing to him, of course. But that was his problem, not mine. I was a rising star, and it was time for the rest of the world to sit up and take notice.

Even back then, I had a knack for getting people to look after me. When I was in high school, my mother still packed me a lunch every day. And if Mom wasn't around or she had to leave early for work, I'd get my sister to do the honors. They did it with all the love in the world, and I was all too happy to let them.

It didn't stop there. I realized I had a talent for getting other people to do things for me. I asked, I demanded, I cajoled. It struck me as perfectly logical: after all, I had to save my energy for cycling. It wasn't all manipulation, though; I always bought presents for my parents and my sister whenever I was abroad. And I gave Floortje the small change from any prize money I won. I brought her along to parties and looked out for her the way a big brother should. And when she turned 18 I bought her a car from the salary I earned with my first professional contract. I did these things out of love, not because I stood to gain or had something to make up for.

In August 2003, I became the Under-23 Dutch time trial champion. It seemed only fitting to me. When we young bloods were given a chance to race the pros at the Ster Elektro Tour and I won the prologue, my reaction was much the same. It was a circuit of around 5 kilometers in Veldhoven, starting and finishing on wet cobbles. I was no hero in the rain: I lumbered around the bends. But I crossed the line with the quickest time of the day, and no one who came after me bettered it. Not even Fabian Cancellara, who finished second. I remember Huub Duyn, a friend who rode for a rival team, looking at the result, realizing I had won, and blurting out, "What the fuck have you done, Thomas?" But it didn't seem like such a big deal to me. It barely dawned on me that I was still only 18.

It was all so easy, so terribly easy. Like throwing sixes with every toss of the dice. As if life was a Sudoku I could solve just by looking at it. Later on in my career, every decision I made was wrong, but for now I was making all the right moves. I did as I pleased, and nothing and no one stood in my way. I lived for cycling, but that's an easy thing to do when you're on a massive winning streak. I was like a dog performing tricks and snapping up treats; every time I put in the effort, the rewards came thick and fast. Under those conditions, training hard is more an addiction than a chore. The setbacks were few—nothing other than an occasional crash: a broken metacarpal in the spring of 2003, losing five teeth while riding in the yellow jersey during the 2004 Tour de l'Avenir. But these were minor upsets along the way. From the word "go," my star was on the rise, with no real misfortunes to ground me.

I may have been one of the youngest riders on the team, but I knew what I was capable of, and I knew what I wanted. We reigned supreme in the Under-23 peloton. We were bursting with talent, and none of our rivals came close. With the likes of Pieter Weening, Koen de Kort, Ryder Hesjedal, Bernhard Kohl, Rory Sutherland, and Laurens ten Dam in our lineup, we could cherry-pick our winners.

I was expected to hold back on occasion to give my fellow riders a shot at victory. Sometimes I obliged, sometimes I didn't. I took three titles in a row—the Tour de Normandie, the Triptyque des Monts et Châteaux, and the Thüringen Rundfahrt—but even so, I seldom sensed any bad blood between me and my teammates. Maybe it was there and I was just oblivious. Or maybe they didn't see me as a direct threat, since it was more or less a given that I was destined for a place among Rabobank's big boys. I was at the top of the pecking order, and in the races I acted accordingly. In the

2003 World Championships in Hamilton, I didn't put in any work for most of the day and only really began to race in the final stages. Together with Markus Fothen I caught the leading group in a single surge to take bronze. Some of the other guys bad-mouthed me for not pulling my weight. I couldn't have cared less—I didn't even try to justify myself. I was setting my own course, and nothing they could say was going to alter that.

As the Rabobank Under-23s, we were given more opportunities to race against the major names. In the spring of 2004 we trained in Portugal and followed that up with the Volta ao Algarve. It was an event I had circled on my calendar; it had been my focus all winter, and I had even gone down there to check out the time trial course. I knew who else would be riding in that race: Lance Armstrong.

By this time Armstrong already had five Tour de France victories to his name, and I was desperate to pit my strength against his. When I rode alongside him during one of the first stages, he struck up a conversation—nothing earth-shattering, just a bit of lighthearted banter. He told me he had already heard stories about me. "I've heard a few about you too," I replied. Truth be told, I was more a fan of Jan Ullrich, but of course it was an honor that a multiple Tour de France winner knew who I was and saw me as a rival. Armstrong held a fascination for me, if only because of his charisma and his entourage. When the pace allowed, I made a point of taking a piss at the side of the road. That meant I got to ride past the U.S. Postal team car as I made my way back to the group and could take a peek at Sheryl Crow, Armstrong's girlfriend at the time, being driven along behind the peloton in the company of director Johan Bruyneel.

Though I managed to reel in seven riders who had started ahead of me in the time trial, I ended up fourth, 19 seconds behind Armstrong. A day later, in a stage with an uphill finish, I went past him. In the general classification I came fourth and he came fifth. Once the Volta was over, the entire peloton headed for the airport. While we mere mortals hopped on our scheduled flights home, Armstrong strolled out to his private jet. I got a real kick out of that: his flair, his showmanship. It was one big act designed to intimidate the rest. He was the gorilla who pounded his chest the loudest. And I was deeply impressed, just as I had been by Nibali and company, the slick Italians I had encountered in my days as a junior.

That combination of cycling and swagger made perfect sense to me. I didn't want to be some faceless chump who happened to go fast on a bike. I wanted to be up there pounding my chest with the other alpha males—on the bike and off it. I wanted the starring role in every show. I didn't have the patience to wait, to take things one step at a time. That year I didn't even consider the Under-23 national time trial championships; I was going to race the pros or not at all. Beforehand I told team director Nico Verhoeven that I would win. And I did.

In the autumn of 2004, along with Rabo teammate Koen de Kort, I was invited to take part in the Grand Prix Eddy Merckx—a two-man time trial in Brussels. For rookies like us, even taking part was an honor; almost all the other two-man teams were established stars. But simply lining up against those big names wasn't enough for me. I wanted more. And I had the power to achieve it. I barely even felt my legs. Koen went through 40 kilometers of hell clinging to my wheel. We caught riders who had started way before us and clocked the fastest time of the day, and none of the teams that followed could match us. Not Erik Dekker and Marc Wauters, not Jens Voigt and Bobby Julich, not Uwe Peschel and Michael Rich, not George Hincapie and Viatcheslav Ekimov. On the podium, Peschel and Rich stood there long-faced and dead-eyed. They felt like they'd been had. The race organizers, commentators, and journalists didn't know what to make of it. Some thought we had taken a shortcut: how in God's name could two snot-nosed kids have beaten all those big names? The accusations were like water off a duck's back. They made me laugh, if anything. Even if it had been possible to cut corners, it would never have occurred to me. Why cut corners when you can win fair and square?

It was the year of the Athens Olympics. Erik Dekker was itching to compete in the time trial, but national coach Gerrie Knetemann passed over him in favor of another Dekker: he selected me. Erik was none too pleased, but for Knetemann it was cut and dried: I was Dutch champion, so the slot was mine.

Fast-forward a few weeks, and there I was at Schiphol with a bright orange suitcase in tow. The heat in Athens was blistering. The tar on the roads was melting, and I was swimming in my own sweat. A bus took me to the Olympic Village. I gave my best tough-guy impersonation, but looking around, it was all I could do to keep my jaw from dropping. The cafeterias were a spectacle in themselves, packed with elite athletes devouring all kinds of food. I turned out to be rooming with another rider. It wasn't until I walked through the door that I saw who it was: Michael Boogerd. That poster of him was still on my bedroom wall back home, and here in Athens he was lying on the bed next to mine. He had run aground in the road race a few days earlier, and now he was taped up like the Michelin Man, bandages and gauze everywhere. I asked him if he was okay. "Course I am, cock!" he beamed. "Crack open that case of yours, lie down, and make yourself at home."

He was a nice guy, but we didn't have a lot to say to each other. Our worlds were so far apart. He was off to a DJ Tiësto concert with Karsten Kroon, while I was obsessing about not being in bed by 10:30. My time trial was nothing to write home about. Perhaps it was unrealistic to expect more. At that age, I just wasn't ready to take on the best in the world at the greatest show on earth. I scraped into the top 20, but it was enough to satisfy Knetemann: "Take a good look around while you still can, son. Next time it'll be yours for the taking."

I was Thomas in Wonderland, a junior playing for the senior team. Up there with the best but with one important difference. I was racing against pros with whopping salaries—even beating them on a good day—yet I was still a rookie with an Under-23 contract to match. In 2003 I was earning €5,000 a year—about $5,800 at that time—though my prize money bumped it up to €25,000.

Since I was riding so fast, I decided to push for a substantial raise in 2004. I felt I had earned it, and before long I found myself sitting next to my dad in a posh restaurant in Breda to negotiate with Jan Raas and Piet Hubert of Rabobank. They were offering €15,000 a year, and I wanted €20,000. Raas and Hubert sent me out into the hall to cool my heels. I paced a hole in the carpet, sitting down and leaping to my feet a hundred times. After what seemed like an age, they called me back in, and we split the difference at €17,500—just over $20,000. I was happy and relieved, but looking back, I reckon they must have had a good chuckle about it afterward. What made them think they had to play hardball with a kid like me for the sake of a few thousand extra? They knew damn well it was peanuts compared with the contracts to come. Maybe they did it to teach me a lesson, to show me you can be happy with a small step up the ladder.

That I would join the Rabobank pro team in 2005 was already set in stone. But 2004 was the year when I got a taste of the real thing. Well into the season, I was given a pro traineeship, riding with the big boys at the Grand Prix de Fourmies, the Rheinland-Pfalz Rundfahrt, and the Coppa Sabatini. It was a test, for the team and for me personally. This was my ticket to another world, the chance to swim out of my depth—still buoyed up by the water wings of my Under-23 contract, but not for long.

7
FIRST SHOT

I STEP INTO THE ROOM, suitcase trailing behind me like an oversized lap dog. There are two beds. One is empty, on the other sits Steven de Jongh, my teammate and roommate for the Rheinland-Pfalz Rundfahrt—my first stage race among the pros. I say hello. He nods at me and flicks channels on the TV. Pay-per-view. I hear groaning and cop an eyeful of pounding flesh. Steven grabs two towels and tosses one my way. "First things first. Time for a wank."

I'm speechless. There I stand, case in hand, coat still on. I'm a trainee. This is my introduction to the pro peloton, my first full week rubbing shoulders with the major names of cycling. I hardly know Steven; I've only really seen him on TV. I've been assigned him as a roommate because he's an experienced rider from the same part of the country as me—a common bond, or so they say. This is the man who's going to tell me what it takes to be a pro. I've been paddling around in the kiddie pool for years; a traineeship with the pro peloton means diving in at the deep end. And riders like Steven are here to keep me afloat. He's a man I look up to. This was not what I imagined when they told me we'd be sharing a room. I thought he'd offer me a friendly hand, not toss me a towel.

I let go of my case, pull down my pants and sit on the bed, doing my best to focus on the on-screen bump and grind. If this is a test, I'm not about to fail it. I want to be part of the gang.

If this is what it takes, then this is what it takes.

A few stages into the race, I receive my first injection from the team doctor one evening. His name is Geert Leinders, a Belgian who's been working for Rabobank for years. He is a smart, reserved man who calmly explains what he is injecting into my body. It's Actovegin, an extract obtained from calf blood. It's not on the doping list but contains amino acids that aid recovery. Leinders asks if I understand. "Of course," I say. To be honest, it's a bit of a kick, a medical man sticking a needle in my arm like that. It all feels very professional.

Strangely enough, the racing itself doesn't differ much from life with the Under-23s. True, there are more good riders, but I don't get ridden into the ground. If anything, it's the opposite. During the second stage, six of us break away on a climb. My teammate Erik Dekker is up there with me and tells me I should focus on picking up points on the mountain stages: "You could be in with a chance of taking the mountain jersey." I'm not impressed. What do I want with the mountain jersey in the Rheinland-Pfalz

Rundfahrt? I'm out to win the stage. And so I don't sprint for the mountain points. Instead I bide my time and launch an attack around 10 kilometers from the finish. No one responds—or no one can respond, who's to say? It's only with the finish line approaching that I look around: the street behind me is empty. I do the decent thing and thrust my hands in the air, but there's no rush of euphoria. I'm not even surprised. I've become so used to winning that this seems normal. There are victory celebrations at dinner that evening. We don't overdo it, a few bottles of wine, that's all. With hindsight I realize how special it was: a young guy like me, a trainee on his first stage race snatching a victory, but then and there it doesn't sink in. When the others tell me what a big deal it is, all I can do is shrug.

After the final stage of Rheinland-Pfalz, in which I finish second, I'm off with the pros to the Coppa Sabatini—an Italian road race that serves as a buildup to the world championships. In the days leading up to the race, I find myself sharing a room with Michael Rasmussen. He comes across as a bit of an oddball. He says next to nothing and would be happier spending every hour of the day alone. He eats next to nothing. I can see his bones through his shirt. A few days before the race we head out for a loop over the Monte Serra. The weather is scorching, but Rasmussen rides with leg warmers and two jackets. He has to "work up a good sweat," he says. At the time I have no idea what he's talking about.

The Coppa Sabatini is a race packed with top riders—Jan Ullrich, Francesco Casagrande, Franco Pellizotti, Stefano Garzelli,

Michael Boogerd—all of them gearing up for the world championships one week later in Verona. Ullrich wins, I come in sixth. I'd
like nothing better than another shot at beating him during the
world championships, but in my determination to become a world
champion, I've opted to compete in the Under-23s. So much for
determination. I beat Vincenzo Nibali in the time trial but still wind
up second to Janez Brajkovič. It's the biggest disappointment of my
career, not least because it hadn't even occurred to me that I might
not win. Up on the podium I have to summon every last ounce of
self-control to stop myself hurling my silver medal to the ground.
And when I get back to the hotel, I sit on the edge of my bed and
sob for minutes on end. A few days later, in the road race, it's second
fucking place again; I make my final move a fraction too late, and it's
not enough to catch breakaway rider Kanstantsin Sivtsov.

That evening I go out on the town with my teammates and my
sister, who has made the trip to Italy to cheer me on. Still choked
with frustration at being double runner-up, I'm hell-bent on
drowning my sorrows. We head for a party at a Verona nightclub
where a lot of the riders are drinking and dancing without a care
in the world; for many it's the end of the season. Mario Cipollini
comes up to me. Not only does he know who I am, but he also
tells me I'm going to be a star and launches into a story about how
good he used to be in his early days. It makes me feel like I belong,
like I'm really making a name for myself in the world of cycling.
It tickles my ego. I can feel how important status is becoming to
me; I long to be recognized, to be acknowledged. I want the major

players to take me seriously. It's the year of my first pro victories. The year the first needle went into my arm. In that nightclub it feels like I have genuinely stepped into another world. My days among the small fry are over. I have ridden my last world championship in the Under-23s. Another peloton awaits, one with a different set of standards.

Late in the evening, I run into Elisa Basso. She's the sister of Ivan Basso, but the two are poles apart: Ivan is a doe-eyed, soft-spoken guy, while Elisa is out there and extroverted. She's beautiful, older than me, part of the official glamour at the world championships. Without a word, she takes me by the hand and steers me through the crowd and out into the night.

8
JACQUES THE MANAGER

HIS HANDSHAKE IS FIRM. His slicked-back hair so black it must be dyed. He's a good talker, a fast talker. Jacques Hanegraaf sits on the couch opposite my parents and me. He has driven all the way to Dirkshorn in his dark Volvo to meet us. He represents riders, negotiates on their behalf. He gives them financial advice and sorts out their taxes. But he has also managed a number of cycling teams, including Farm Frites and Team Coast. He knows everyone in cycling, and everyone in cycling knows him.

It was national coach Gerrie Knetemann who put me in touch with Jacques. Gerrie reckoned I could use a manager to sort out the paperwork and the finances, leaving me to concentrate on the sporting side of my career. He recommended Hanegraaf with the best of intentions. "A slippery character, but he knows what he's doing."

It's November 2004 when Jacques pays us a visit. We move from the couch to the dining room table. I'm drinking Fanta; he and my parents are sipping coffee. I'm nervous. I can't put my finger on it, but something about him makes me feel uneasy. He talks all evening. He spins a good yarn. He tells us I'm extremely talented, that it's only a matter of time before I'm winning the biggest races in the world. But, he cautions, that level of success brings commitments. Being a pro is not just about training, eating, sleeping, and racing—there are a host of other matters that need tending. Negotiations with team managers, sponsorship contracts, media—you name it. I need people in place to support me. I need someone I can count on no matter what. And that someone is Jacques Hanegraaf.

He wins me over, and my parents right along with me. He promises me the earth, plays on my ambitions, convincing me that I'm already a major catch. Every team would be happy to have me, the man of the future. Rabobank should thank their lucky stars that I'm willing to ride for them. And, Jacques insists, nothing says gratitude like cold, hard cash: An exceptional rider like me should be earning at least €200,000 in his first year as a pro. That's about $250,000. He's pushing all the right buttons; it's exactly what I want to hear. He builds me up, makes me feel like I matter. I decide to take the plunge and have him represent me. I give him the go-ahead to set about extracting €200,000 from the powers that be.

There's only one problem: In May I signed a two-year contract with Rabobank for the 2005 and 2006 seasons at an annual salary of €100,000. Daylight robbery according to Jacques, and he talks me into believing that I shouldn't stand for it, that we should try to break open the contract. I don't need much convincing. When I signed on the dotted line it seemed like a shitload of money, but Jacques has fanned the flames of discontent, and the heat has flipped a switch. I'm playing with the grown-ups now, a whole different ball game compared with quaking in my boots as I drove down to Breda with my dad to ask for a couple grand more. This is the big time, and €100,000 isn't going to cut it. My parents look on bewildered. To them, a hundred grand is a fortune, especially for a young guy like me. But they've already lost their hold on me. I am not like them. I see nothing wrong with wanting more. By the time Jacques slides behind the wheel of his Volvo and takes off into the night, he's already driven a wedge between me and Rabobank.

More, more, more—there was always a feeling of dissatisfaction in me, but up to this point it was a flicker that burned a little brighter once in a while. As my manager, Jacques sparks a raging fire. He and I have our own way of counting: $1 + 1 = 3$. I want money and he wants money. Of everything I earn—salary, bonuses, starting fees—he receives 10 percent plus tax. And we are not ones to bide our time. With Jacques it's not about long-term strategy. We never talk about where I will be in 5 or 10 years' time. Patience is for losers. Waiting is for duds. We don't have the time to sit back and see how my first few years as a pro pan out. We want the spoils and we want them now.

I move to Belgium not long after, on Jacques's advice. A little place called Lanaken, just over the border from Maastricht. It's home to more than a few Dutch riders, offering better terrain for training and a far more attractive tax climate.

Jacques sets about trying to break open my Rabobank contract before it has officially begun. He proposes doubling my salary from €100,000 to €200,000, but Theo de Rooij, who has succeeded Jan Raas as director, is not impressed. He insists that I've signed a contract and that €100,000 is plenty for a lad of 20. First things first—they want to see how I handle my first full season as a pro. Hanegraaf is livid and so am I. I feel unappreciated. Who do those Rabo execs think they are? Bunch of penny-pinching bastards.

I'm still a kid. I've just munched my way through a family pack of potato chips, and I want more. And if I don't get it, I'll start whining. It's not enough; it'll never be enough. That craving for more is working its way into my system. I've become infected.

A chronic case of discontent.

9
INITIATION

IT'S A MEAT MARKET. The girls come up one by one and introduce themselves, names that could have been copied from the latest porn flick. They're strutting around on stilettos, skirts so short you only have to tilt your head to see what's underneath. One dizzying look into their plunging necklines and we're all standing at attention.

There's a bunch of us at the bar, all of us riders. We knock back beer and Bacardis and discuss who's going to have which girl. I'm excited, but this feels awkward and uncomfortable at the same time. It's my first ever trip to a brothel. The name of the club is Sauna Diana, not far from the hotel where we're stationed for our first winter training camp. It's early December 2004—not long now till my first pro season.

It hasn't taken me long to work out that training with the Rabobank pros is a world away from the Under-23s or the juniors.

I thought it would be more serious, but the opposite is true. There's more to the lifestyle than cycling alone, and a pro training camp is a game of two halves. By day we ride our mountain bikes over muddy woodland tracks; by night we break out the booze. In the preceding years, I swore off alcohol altogether between January 1 and October 1. Except for the party after the Dutch championships, I wouldn't touch a drop and thought I was pushing my luck if I had even a couple of nights out in winter, especially if there was a heavy training session in store next day. Life with the pros is different: It's wine with dinner every evening, followed by a drinking session in the bar. If riders take off for the night, no one seems that bothered. It's all par for the course, apparently. It doesn't even occur to me to say no when Michael Boogerd invites me along to a brothel. I'm honored to be asked. Before I know it, there we are, five of us crammed into a car, next stop Sauna Diana. The Siemons brothers who own the place greet us at the door. They know everyone by name.

The girl of my choice is more a woman. Around 40 is my guess. She's blonde, and she's nice to me. At the time it hardly registers that I've singled out a woman who's 20 years my senior, but looking back now it makes sense: I often fall for older women. We take a swim for half an hour or so, and then we go up to a room. Once the deed is done, I wander back down to find the other guys waiting for me in the bar. We settle up and drive back to the hotel. Next morning it's back to the mud and the woods.

The winter before my first pro season is one training camp after another. And between the team camps I head off to Mallorca on my own and train like mad every day, putting in 35 or 40 hours a week. I'm brimming over with ambition, determined to make my mark from the very first race.

At the Rabobank training camps in Spain, I am one of the best. On the test runs up the Coll de Rates, I leave everyone in my tracks. But I don't want to fall short of the mark at night either: I'm there for every drinking session. Pinballing between one extreme and the other, I notice that I'm as full-on about my drinking as I am about my cycling. I develop a taste for wine, but mostly I knock back the hard stuff with sugary mixers. We go out to sleazy Spanish bars that pack in the summer tourists but in winter have to make do with an unruly bunch of track-suited riders and the odd stray drunk. We drink, we slur, sing, talk bullshit, get chucked out, throw up behind bus shelters, and stagger back to the hotel, drunk as farts. Yet the training sessions are fast and furious, and more often than not, it's the hardest drinkers who set the pace. No one gives an inch; your macho status depends on how fast you ride and how you hold your drink. Hung over or not, everyone's up and ready for training at 10:00 on the dot. No one comes late. Except for Óscar Freire. But then he's late for everything.

After training one afternoon, I'm walking back to my room when I hear footsteps pounding down the corridor behind me. I look round to see a bunch of teammates stampeding in my direction. I can't make out who exactly; they've all got tighty-whities or stockings pulled over their heads. The runt of the litter—so scrawny it could only be Michael Rasmussen behind the underpants mask—is brandishing a hair trimmer. I know what this is. I've already heard the tall tales about past initiations, but I'm not parting with my long hair for anyone. I try to escape, but there are too many of them, and before I know it, they've grabbed me and dragged me into a room. "Don't struggle, Thomas," one of them yells. "It's all in the game!" But I thrash and kick for all I'm worth. No fucking way am I leaving this room bald as a coot. I get wilder and wilder, and there's nothing they can do to pin me down. Eventually they give up. Puffing and panting, Marc Wauters pulls the stocking from his head and sits down on the bed. "If you're not willing to be initiated, how do you expect us to ride for you in the races?" he asks. "Initiation has nothing to do with it," I reply. "Rabobank is paying you to ride for me."

There were no initiations that year. All of us newbies escaped with our hair intact.

10

A BOOST
FOR THE WORLDS

THE FRIDAY BEFORE MY FIRST PARIS–NICE, I stay at Erik Dekker's house in Meerle. Same surname, no relation. The team thinks he might make a good mentor for his up-and-coming namesake. Like me, he's a time trialist, and he rides fast in the classics—just like I want to. At the training camps and after races, he can sometimes be a bit boisterous, but he seldom gives much away. It makes me all the more interested in what he has to say.

I sleep in the spare room. Erik's wife hands me the bedclothes and says goodnight. I make up the bed and climb in, but as I pull the covers over me, the edge of the sheet catches between my little toe and the one next to it. I tear open the skin, and immediately the blood starts flowing. It won't stop. Red stains spread across the clean white sheets. I don't know what to do. I can hardly wake the great Erik Dekker whining like a kid that I've cut my toe. Thank

Christ I find a little plastic bag in the room. I slip it around my bleeding foot and manage to get some sleep. The next day I have to explain the bloodbath to Erik and his wife. Luckily they see the funny side. My relief is tangible.

The team picks us up at Erik's place, and we room together for the whole week. I natter away to him, but he's a good bit less talkative in return. His main focus is on himself. One night after we've settled down in our beds, I ask Erik what the deal is with doping. I wasn't born yesterday, I read the papers, and I know fellow riders are using. I also know that Erik was barred from competing in the world championships a few years earlier because his hematocrit—the percentage of blood that contains red blood cells—was too high, a standard indicator of blood doping. But apart from that it's just hearsay, a world away from my own cycling experience. "Doping" is a magic word from a parallel universe, far away yet very close at the same time.

Erik refuses to discuss it. "Listen, Thomas, you're a nice guy, and I'm happy to share a room with you, but we are not going to talk about doping. Not now, not ever. You will never hear a word on that subject from me." As statements go, this one is pretty damn clear.

That week I take sleeping pills for the first time. What was unthinkable for the Under-23s turns out to be common practice for the pros. On race days the doctor does two rounds: one round after the stage to administer a drip with vitamins, minerals, and other perfectly legal substances to boost recovery, and one round in the evening to hand out sleeping pills. A few riders pass them up, but most of us take them. Michael Boogerd pops a pill on a daily basis, says he can't sleep without them. Knowing he takes them, and because I like the idea of dropping off to sleep straightaway, I take them too.

Where Erik Dekker is a closed book, Michael Boogerd is much more open. While Dekker slams the door to the dark side of cycling resolutely in my face, Boogerd leaves it ajar. It's not like Michael starts reeling off the names of every substance he's ever used, but he doesn't shy away from talk of pills or even injections. Michael and I have hit it off by this time. We laugh at the same things, listen to the same music, eye up the same women, and we both love cycling with the same intensity. Ask him who came sixth in the Giro dell'Emilia five years ago, and he doesn't even have to think before he answers. Like me, he does things to excess. When he trains, he goes deep. And when he drinks, he drinks hard.

I hold my own in the races. I muddle through Paris–Nice with a heavy cold, but one week later, in the Critérium International, I'm up there with the best of them. In the second stage, a morning ride of 90 kilometers, the race is on from the very start. The weather is filthy—wet roads under darkened skies. Before I know where I am, a group of favorites have made a break for it: Jens Voigt, Jörg Jaksche, Bobby Julich, and Ivan Basso. In the peloton, a small space opens up on the right of the road. I seize my chance, put in a solitary spurt, and latch on to the leaders. The peloton sets off in pursuit, but they don't stand a chance. Our break is the equivalent of a team time trial, and my legs don't protest once. It's a modest uphill finish. Jaksche makes his play, but he's much too early. I wait till the right moment and sprint past him to take the stage. It's my first big-time victory, but again it hardly makes a dent on my consciousness. After the finish, I'm more concerned about the actual time trial later the same day. I want to be top of the general classification too, but that's out of reach. I finish fourth in the time trial—behind Jens Voigt, but well up on the likes of Bradley Wiggins and Floyd Landis. It's enough for second overall, but for me that's one place too low. I'm pissed off about my time trial, pissed off that I didn't win.

In the spring I spend €600 on vitamins and fish oil. They arrive in a big cardboard box. Michael Boogerd and Steven de Jongh see me lugging it down the hotel corridor and ask me what's in it. When I tell them vitamins and fish oil, they nearly piss themselves laughing. I don't get it. There's me thinking I'm making a wise investment in my physical fitness, and Boogerd and De Jongh are splitting their sides. When they finally catch their breath, Michael says, "For that kind of money you could have ridden a whole lot faster." A sheepish chuckle is all I can muster.

The Giro d'Italia is my first major tour. I am going there to learn, to gain wisdom and experience for the years ahead. On the two long time trials I want to pit myself against the best in the world. On the other stages I decide to play it day by day and take my chances as they come. Rabobank has no clear-cut leading rider at this point. Before the start in Reggio Calabria, deep in the south of Italy, the team is buzzing with a rumor that one of our Russians,

Alexandr Kolobnev, has had a sky-high hematocrit test. From then on he has to fly back to Holland before every race to have it checked by the team. There are also whispers that the Italian police plan to raid the riders' hotels in search of doping. The Rabobank team managers decide to play it safe and confiscate all our supplements, even my expensive vitamins. Instead we have to make do with a single Supradyn multivitamin a day.

As the stages progress, I feel a world of difference between the Giro and the races earlier in the season. The pace is so quick it's unreal, especially on the climbs. For the first time in years, I'm cut right down to size, reduced to making up the numbers in the peloton. In the lesser races I have the measure of the best riders, but in the Giro those same guys leave me choking in their dust. I hang on and hang on, but as soon as the real contenders put their foot on the accelerator, I'm blown away like a daisy in a mountain gale. At mealtimes and in the team bus we talk about the speed on display. The hints being dropped about the top riders aren't exactly subtle. The cynical way senior teammates remark that Ivan Basso is "in really good form" speaks volumes. I see Basso in the races but only from a distance, way, way ahead of me. I see his sister at much closer quarters; after two weeks of texting, Elisa pays me a visit. By this time I've spent time with quite a few women, but Elisa's company is confirmation of my newfound status, and I'm flattered.

In the final week of the Giro, I'm hanging on for grim death with nothing but a mouthful of ulcers to show for my pain. After three punishing mountain stages in succession, I stand there weeping in the shower, barely able to stand. Suddenly I feel like a very little boy in a big man's world. The years leading up to this point were so easy. Not once did I have to settle for a place in the grupetto—my career path was heading straight for glory. Here in the Giro is where it grinds to a halt.

In hindsight I know it all made sense; you can't expect a pro in his first year to withstand the rigors of a major tour. And it could have been a whole lot worse. I can't keep up with the best on the climbs, but I never have trouble coming in on time, and I don't struggle nearly as much as the half of the peloton that finishes behind me. But as an eager young gun of 20, I have trouble seeing the bright side.

Bitterly disappointed, I go in search of explanations, and I hit upon doping as one of the main reasons the leading climbers are leaving me for dead. That experience in the Giro lays the foundations for my conviction that without resorting to banned substances, the prizes that matter will always be out of reach. After one of the toughest mountain stages yet, I collapse into a seat on the team bus and pour my heart out to Frans Maassen, one of the team managers. I complain fiercely that it's doping that's making the pace so ruthless. "I mean, it's humanly impossible, isn't it?" The conversation turns sour within seconds. Maassen snaps that I've no right to make unfounded doping accusations and that I should stop whimpering.

I don't have a bad word to say about Frans Maassen. In all the years I've known him, I've never heard him say a word about doping, and the story goes that he cut short his own cycling career rather than resort to the blood-boosting drug EPO. Looking back, part of me understands why he didn't want to talk to me about doping, but at the time I can't just pretend it doesn't exist. I'm too curious. I need to talk to people about it, people who are on my side. And there are no such people on the Rabobank pro team. There is no policy. There is no guidance. The managers act as if doping doesn't exist while most of the riders make their own arrangements. I take orders from the team managers in the race, but I don't look up to them. They don't seem to understand what I'm going through, what I need.

And so I go in search of other role models, other points of reference. And I find them in the riders around me, especially the leading riders who are pushing the pace. Allowing myself to be drawn to the wrong examples is my own fault, my own weakness. But from the vantage point I have today, I would have killed for a big name in my own team who had the backbone to look me in the eye and tell me to keep my fucking paws off the dope.

At the end of my first pro year, I travel from the Eneco Tour, where I finish fourth, to the Tour de Pologne. The accommodation's top-notch, five-star comfort every night. The Polish hotel near Karpacz where we find ourselves after one of the mountain stages is no exception. I'm rooming with Joost Posthuma, and we're both bored out of our skulls. I suggest nipping down to the bar for a Coke.

There turns out to be a half-decent attempt at a nightclub in the basement. I can't believe my eyes: gorgeous women wall to wall. It's

like we've gate-crashed a Victoria's Secret convention. The super-
models turn out to be hookers. I signal to a girl to see if she's up for
it. She gives me the nod. I warn Joost that he'll have to put off his
beauty sleep for a while, and I take her up in the elevator and down
the long corridor to our room. We're almost in the door when I spot
Erik Breukink in the distance. He's a key figure on the management
team and the man in charge during the Tour de Pologne. I hope he
has somehow missed the sight of me shoving a leggy blonde into
the room ahead of me. Fat chance; a minute later I hear a knock at
the door. I peer through the peephole and swear under my breath.
Of course, Breukink is standing at the door. I nudge the Polish girl
and put my finger to my lips. "Shhh!" I bundle her into the toilet
and open the door to the room. Breukink storms in. "I know you
have a girl in here! Where the hell is she?" I act as if I haven't a clue
what he's talking about. He takes a look on the balcony, peers under
the bed, then he checks the toilet and finds my hidden treasure. His
face turns bright red, and blotches appear on his neck. Just short of
foaming at the mouth, he shoves the girl out into the hallway and
climbs on his soapbox. "For fuck's sake, Thomas! Who do you think
you are? You have a race tomorrow." It goes in one ear and out the
other. I have to bite my lip not to laugh when he adds, "And at your
age too. When you still have everything to prove. Michael Boogerd
and Erik Dekker would never pull a stunt like this." Maybe he honestly doesn't know. But I take it as proof that he has no idea what's
going on in his own team. Either that or he doesn't want to know.
And why should I pay any heed to a guy like that?

The next day there's a time trial on the menu, an early start. I avoid looking Breukink in the eye at breakfast. He's clearly still mad at me. I don't dare look at my teammates either, for fear I'll burst out laughing. It's a bit like being back at school, playing dumb when the teacher's been hit on the back of the head by a spitball.

As a kind of disciplinary measure I have to ride the time trial without a manager in the team car. With no expert guidance, I'm left to rely on the encouragement of one of the soigneurs, Ton van Engelen. It's all the same to me. I'll ride till my lungs are ready to burst anyway. I outpace them all and win the time trial—ahead of Bobby Julich—and end up third in the general classification, my first podium placing in a ProTour race.

I have to take a doping test, and Breukink accompanies me. We sit there next to each other in the cubicle till it's my turn. I say nothing. Breukink says nothing. A good 10 minutes pass before he mutters, "If you'd behaved yourself last night, you could've won the whole damned thing." I let my silence do the talking.

That year's world championships are held in Madrid. It's hot and dusty. I am riding for the national squad, but a Rabobank doctor is part of the delegation: Geert Leinders. The day before the road race he comes to my room carrying a syringe and a small bottle. It says Synacthen on the label. I don't know what it is, but I've heard the word before, in conversations at the dinner table. Leinders explains that it boosts the body's own cortisone production. He tells me I might feel a little inhibited to begin with, but it can give me a surge of euphoria toward the end of a long race and help me dig deeper. It's not a miracle drug, but it might help. As part of his spiel, he drops in the fact that it's on the list of banned substances, adding immediately that it's untraceable. The drawback with cortisone is water retention, so I need to make sure I wrap up well for my warm-up. "That'll give you the chance to sweat it out."

The cortisone injection doesn't feel like doping. I don't feel like I'm crossing any kind of line. During the race, I don't notice much of a difference. I stick to the back of the peloton all day, work my way through in the final stages, and I'm the only one who can go with Alejandro Valverde when he bridges the gap to the leading group. I end up 15th, a result I'm only moderately pleased with.

Later on a whole peloton of cyclists hits the nightlife in Madrid. I drink so much that the entire night is a blur, except for Tom Boonen managing to lose his newly won rainbow jersey in some club or other. I arrive back at the hotel completely shitfaced.

11

THE COACH

I HAVE THREE SETS OF PARENTS. There's Mom and Dad, of course, and two other older couples I see as foster parents in a way. The first is Kees and Karien—a well-to-do couple who live in the town of Luyksgestel in the Dutch province of Brabant. They are cycling fans, attend all the local races, and like to give the riders they know a helping hand. Dirk Bellemakers—one of my best friends and a pro with a number of Belgian teams—often pays them a visit. Kees owns a metalwork company that has been sponsoring a women's cycling team for years.

In the summer of 2003, my dad gets talking to Kees and Karien at a cycling race, and they tell him I should call if I'm ever racing in their neck of the woods and need a place to stay. I take them up on the offer in August that same year when I ride the Under-23 national time trial championships. I'm a bit bashful about the whole thing; turning up on someone's doorstep to bed down for the night isn't something I do every day. But Kees and Karien make me feel right at home.

In the years that follow I become a son of sorts; Kees already has two sons from a previous marriage. For racing and training camps, Luyksgestel is often a better base than Dirkshorn, and rattling around my apartment in Lanaken gets a bit lonely sometimes, so I often sleep over at Kees and Karien's. We have breakfast together, I read the paper, play with their grandkids, and head out from there on my training rides. They follow every detail of my career, regularly accompany me to races and comb the sports pages in search of my name. Kees even polishes my bike.

Maybe I gravitate toward Kees and Karien because I'm not the kid I once was. The world around me is changing, and I am changing with it. If I talk to my parents back in Dirkshorn about money and fast cars, it's like I've been beamed down from another planet. With Kees and Karien it all feels more comfortable. Kees is extroverted, and like me, he has a love of sports cars. But it's much more than just filling up a lonely life with car talk and an omelet for breakfast. Kees and Karien are among the kindest people I know. They have helped me out of so many ridiculous scrapes. All these years down the line, I can honestly say that without them I wouldn't be standing here today. More of that later.

In 2006, a third set of parents enters my life, the Cecchinis. Luigi Cecchini is a cycling coach, one of the finest in the world.

Before I met him he worked with Bjarne Riis, Jan Ullrich, and Michele Bartoli, and when I make his acquaintance he has riders like Alessandro Petacchi and Tyler Hamilton under his wing. After the 2005 World Championships I fly to Pisa with Jacques Hane-graaf for an initial meeting. Jacques has made all the arrangements; he knows Cecchini from his time as manager of Team Coast, where Jan Ullrich had been the star rider.

Luigi Cecchini is around 60 at the time and looks every inch the Italian aristocrat, class oozing from every pore. His gray hair is trimmed to perfection, and his clothes are just as immaculate—inconspicuous but expensive. The glasses he wears subtly accentuate his authority. He speaks calmly, never once raises his voice. He doesn't have to. He speaks, and everyone in the room listens.

He has taken an interest in me. He has noted my results and sees the fire in my eyes. But he is only willing to train me if I am good enough, if my engine packs enough power. Cecchini only coaches riders for his own pleasure. He has more money than he knows what to do with, and he and his wife own half of Lucca. Before he decides whether to take me on, I will be put to the test.

We drive to Monte Serra, south of Lucca. Cecchini's instructions are simple: Ride to the top as fast as you can. Stopwatch in hand, he follows me up in a Smart car. When I reach the top, he gives me a brief chance to catch my breath before the next challenge, a five-minute all-out exertion test designed to measure my power output. He looks at the results and whistles through his teeth. The old master is impressed. I will be allowed to train with him. And pay €5,000 a year for the privilege. That said, to this day he has never charged me a single cent for his services.

Rabobank is far from happy with my choice. Cecchini is a man with a reputation; some of the riders he has worked with have been subject to doping allegations, and the Italian authorities have investigated him for involvement in facilitating doping, though he has never been sanctioned. Theo de Rooij asks me if I would consider an alternative. I tell him no, and that's the end of it. When asked about it in interviews, I point out that Rabobank can't stop me from making my own choices. And if they try, I'll just have to find myself another team. I couldn't care less about Cecchini's image. I want the best coach, and that's all there is to it. Doping is no reason for me to work or not to work with someone. It doesn't scare me off. Personally I have never seen anything to justify Cecchini's dodgy image. In all the years I trained with him, he never once suggested that I dope. Besides, by that time I'd found my own contacts.

I move to Italy so I can train with Cecchini on a daily basis. Some days he joins me on the bike, on others he rides ahead of me on a scooter or behind me in a car. In the first months of 2006 I live at Hotel Caesar in Lido di Camaiore. The owner is an avid cycling fan and offers me a room where I can stow my equipment for months on end, though he only accepts payment when I'm there—€50 a day. My training sessions with Cecchini—"Cecco" for short—continue, and I begin to reap the rewards.

At the end of January, we do another test on Monte Serra. Along with Alessandro Petacchi and Tyler Hamilton, we ride to the foot of the climb in Buti. It's cold, and piles of snow linger at the side of the road, but every fiber of my being is raring to go. I am psyched up and race ready. I fly up the mountain, leaving Alessandro and Tyler far behind and reaching the top in 16 minutes and 30 seconds, with an average wattage of 493. Cecco is impressed; it's one of the fastest times he's ever clocked, beaten only by Jan Ullrich and Francesco Casagrande. He's jumping for joy, and I can't make head or tail of the excited sentences he's firing off in Italian. I've never seen him so enthusiastic.

I become a more regular house guest at the Cecchinis'. I talk to Luigi about cycling and learn to speak Italian. Signora Cecchini cooks for me and soon starts referring to me as *nostro figlio olandese*. Our son from Holland. Their own son, Stefano, becomes a friend from the start. We eat out together, watch football together, go out on the town and get drunk together, and purchase stock for the fashion store he owns in the center of Lucca. We have the same taste: expensive. I have no problem shelling out €600 for a pair of jogging pants. As long as they're cashmere.

I suppose there are reasons why I have families wherever I go. I crave company. I can't do without fathers and mothers. It sometimes feels like this body houses more than one Thomas Dekker. There's the arrogant, self-assured man of the world who throws his money around. A guy who knows what he wants and who speaks Italian with the Italians. But there's also the insecure little boy from

Dirkshorn who is a long, long way from home. Who doesn't know what to do with himself when he's alone. Who has never cooked a meal or even bought his own groceries. Who wants his mother to pack his suitcase and his sister to make his sandwiches. And who hasn't a fucking clue how to look after himself.

12
THE TERRITORY

THE APPETIZERS HAVE JUST ARRIVED. Mom and Dad are sitting at one side of the table, Jacques Hanegraaf and I at the other. Jacques has invited them for a luxurious meal at The Golden Angel in Schagen.

It's all small talk at first—the weather, their jobs, my latest races. Then, between one forkful and the next, he puts his cards on the table. "There's something I want to talk to you about." He says it casually, as if he's about to recommend a film or the special offers at the supermarket that's just opened around the corner. Instead, Jacques tells them I'm brimming with talent and have put in a fantastic first pro season but that it takes more than that to reach the top. He explains that all the top riders are playing a grown-up game and that it's time for me to join in. "Everyone's in on it," he says. "It comes with the territory." Rather than use the word "doping," he dishes up one cryptic description after another.

I say nothing. I knew that Jacques was going to break it to my parents. We discussed it a few weeks beforehand. It was time for the next step, he said, and it didn't take much to win me over. I wasn't blind. I could feel how much faster the pace was in the big races, speed that couldn't simply be due to training hard and getting enough sleep.

As the years went by I could feel it coming. I knew doping would cross my path. And when it happened I did not back away. It came step by step: first a drip to aid recovery, then cortisone injections. The night before this meal I had taken speed and Ecstasy at a rave in Ghent with Michael Boogerd and Steven de Jongh. Both drugs can trip you up if you're tested, but these are the days before out-of-competition checks. The next step—to banned performance-enhancing substances—is only a baby step for me.

Riding as a junior and an amateur, it never entered my mind, but the seed was planted with my transition to the pro circuit. That seed took root, and during my first year as a pro it grew and flowered. I gave it water, the riders around me watered it too. The realization that doping was necessary grew and grew. Without doping I was a good rider, but not good enough. And for me there's no such thing as enough. It's like dancing with a pretty girl; I can't help but look over her shoulder to see if a prettier girl has just walked through the door.

While Jacques does the talking, I watch my mother's face. There's a crease between her eyebrows. Her lips are pressed tight. I see panic in her eyes. When Jacques has said his piece, she looks at me, and she can see that I've already made my choice. If my parents had told me not to dope, I would have laughed in their faces. My father is speechless. My mother whispers, "I only hope this turns out okay."

After dinner, Jacques gets back into his car and drives off, leaving us with the bill. Looking back, there is something surreal about that evening. It's as if Jacques was asking my parents' permission. As if part of him realized you can't simply let a 21-year-old rider enter the world of doping without some kind of public acknowledgment in advance. But at the time it all strikes me as perfectly natural. I believe Jacques has my best interests at heart. We both want the same thing: to reach the top as quickly as possible—more victories, more money. Jacques succeeds in renegotiating my contract with Rabobank, and my salary finally goes up to €400,000 a year, excluding bonuses. That's a bit over $500,000. Ten percent of that amount—plus VAT—is for Jacques.

He has found a goose to lay him golden eggs. Its name is Thomas Dekker.

13

YOUR BLOOD IS YOUR BLOOD

JACQUES KNOWS HIS DOPE. He knows what's on the market, what works, and what doesn't. And he knows what style of doping offers the least chance of getting caught: blood transfusion. He tells me the big names in the pro peloton have been doing it for years and that he even experimented with it himself in his days as a rider. Aranesp, EPO, and CERA—which is third-generation EPO, basically—are all traceable to a greater or lesser degree, but your own blood is your own blood. It's impossible for any doping control to detect, Jacques insists. He talks about Jan Ullrich, who used blood doping in the 2003 Tour de France.

First Jacques tries to find a Dutch doctor willing to tap my blood and freeze it, but this proves impossible to arrange. In Holland, all blood bags are marked and registered; obtaining them for unofficial purposes is no easy feat. And so Jacques gets in touch with an old acquaintance: Eufemiano Fuentes, the man who helped Jan Ullrich arrange his blood doping in the days when Jacques was his teammate. Today the name Fuentes is widely known, but at the start of 2006 only a select few know what he is up to. He never seeks the spotlight, a phantom hovering in the shadows behind sport's bright façade.

I first meet Fuentes on February 10, 2006, the day after the final stage of the Vuelta a Mallorca. By coincidence Rabobank has booked me a flight with a transfer in Madrid. With four hours to while away at Barajas Airport and secure in the knowledge that my bags are being sent on to Pisa, I head out through customs with only my hand luggage. I hail a cab and give the driver the name of the hotel where we have agreed to meet: the Diana TRYP Hotel, 2 kilometers from the airport.

When I enter the lobby, Fuentes and Hanegraaf are ready and waiting. I walk over, shake hands, and collapse into an armchair. I order a soda from the waitress. Fuentes looks like a million other Spaniards his age. Trousers neatly pressed, hair neatly parted, open-necked shirt, and a pair of the brown suede loafers that are a staple of every shoe shop in Madrid. He speaks broken English. His repertoire includes "hello" and just about stretches to rudimentary chit-chat, but when we get down to the business of what kind of doping he can arrange, he switches to Spanish. I don't speak a word of Spanish, but Jacques does. They speak calmly and evenly; I sit and watch them. Every now and then, Jacques translates something for me.

Fuentes has a whole range of dope on offer. You can go to him for EPO, growth hormones, and testosterone. He can help you out with an extensive regime of day-by-day and week-by-week advice on what you should be taking and when. But Jacques and I are only interested in blood transfusion, to keep the risk of being caught to an absolute minimum. I don't want to mess around trying to inject myself with everything under the sun. I go for the most expensive, medically advanced, and least traceable form of doping. No half-assed shenanigans—this is all or nothing.

The idea behind it is simple: You give blood, which is then stored. The body responds to the lack of blood in your system and shifts gear in the days that follow to compensate for the blood loss. You feel a bit weak at the knees for a while but in 7 to 10 days it's as if nothing's happened. When the blood is reinfused at a later date, your blood volume increases. And more blood means more red blood cells, which means improved oxygen transport. As a result, you can generate more power and need less time to recover between races.

The best results are achieved by reinfusing the blood just before the start of a major race or during a stage race. The benefits in a grand tour are enormous. While the blood values of your competitors are dropping steadily, a transfusion in the third week gives you the edge. It's like refueling. Pop in a blood bag, and before you know it you're fit as a fiddle again.

In the past, riders sometimes used other people's blood, often donated by family members. But by 2006 that's been traceable for some time; anti-doping sleuths can find the donor's DNA in your bloodstream. Stick to your own blood and there's no problem. After all, how is anyone supposed to spot the difference between your own blood and your own blood?

Fuentes has two systems to choose from, one short-term, one long-term. The short system involves withdrawing blood and keeping it in the fridge for up to a month at a temperature of around 39 degrees Fahrenheit. In the long system, the tapped blood is frozen and can be stored for years. The smartest thing to do is give blood in the winter months when you're not racing. I'm too late for that; the season is already under way, and I have my sights firmly set on an early victory in the Tirreno–Adriatico, an Italian stage race in March.

We come up with the following plan: I will give blood for the first time that same day, one bag of 450 milliliters to be stored in the fridge for the short system. In a few weeks' time, ahead of the Tirreno–Adriatico, Fuentes will return it to my bloodstream. After that we will tap more blood, to be frozen ready for use during the next Tour de France. The price for storing blood bags in Fuentes's freezer is €10,000, cash only. We agree that I will pay him later in the year.

While Fuentes and Hanegraaf run through the details, tossing the odd snatch of translation my way, I take a look around, and my mind starts to wander. Here we are discussing blood bags as if they are salads on the lunch menu. Tourists with backpacks mill around, and businessmen stroll by with their mobiles clamped to their ears. I cast an approving glance at the rear of a tasty steward-ess who sashays past in high heels. Something in me knows we are playing a cheating game, but that's not how it feels. It feels more like being admitted to a secret brotherhood that everybody knows exists, only no one knows where the clubhouse is or who exactly is a member.

I finish my Coke, and Fuentes gets to his feet and nods in my direction. "Vamos, Thomas," he says, pointing at the ceiling. "Come, come." I get up and follow him to the elevator. He pushes the button, and we start to ascend. We stand side by side in uncom-fortable silence, watching the little light jump from floor to floor. The elevator shudders to a halt. Fuentes steps out into the corridor and stops at one of the doors. He takes a card from his pocket, slides it into the lock, and disappears inside. I hesitate for a second and look over my shoulder to see if there's anyone watching. Then I cross the threshold.

The room is a thousand shades of dark.

14
NO WORRIES

I SLOUCH IN MY SEAT, cap pulled low over my eyes. I have already removed the SIM card from my phone; today and tomorrow I'll be off the grid. Hardly anyone knows where I'm going. My parents, my sister, my team—they're all in the dark. Only Jacques Hanegraaf knows that I am on this flight, heading for Spain to keep an appointment with Eufemiano Fuentes.

It's March 4, 2006, the Saturday before the Tirreno–Adriatico. A few days earlier I texted Fuentes on a prepaid phone bought specifically to contact him. One line, that was all. A greeting in English followed by my arrival time in Madrid. Then came a number. My number: 24. I pressed send. A few minutes later I received a reply, "OK," by way of confirmation followed by the name of the hotel where we are to meet. Same as last time, the Diana TRYP Hotel, close to the airport. The drill is the same too, only in reverse. This time the blood will be flowing into my body, not draining from it.

The plane is packed with holidaymakers and businessmen. The women in the seats in front of me are chatting about the weather in Tuscany. Next to me a man in a suit is banging away at his laptop. I gaze out of the window at the earth below and think about the bag of blood that's waiting for me in Madrid. I'm on edge, but it's not a knife-edge. I feel like everything's under control, and it occurs to me that I am good at this game. Weighing up my actions, steering clear of pitfalls. Never texting Fuentes on my own phone or talking out of turn. I wonder whether I could have been a criminal in another life. The answer is more yes than no.

It's late in the evening when my plane touches down at Barajas. I catch a cab to the hotel. Fuentes has texted me the room number. I walk through the lobby and along the hotel corridors without making eye contact with anyone. I reach the room and knock on the door. Fuentes opens it, and I step inside. It's the same setup as last time. Standard room, dark, curtains drawn, a shiny spread on the bed. We exchange no more than a word or two. It's clear we have nothing to say to each other. I sense that he is totally indifferent to who I am or what I do. I am a number, nothing more. And I'm not the only one. I'm number 24, which means there must be at least 23 others.

Fuentes takes a bag of blood from the backpack next to him. He shows it to me and points at the number. "Check this please," he says. I see the number and recognize my handwriting. I nod. He removes a picture from the wall—another random floral print—and hangs the blood bag from the nail. I take off my jacket and lie down on the bed. Fuentes begins to clean the inside of my arm with a wad of cotton dipped in Betadine. He takes his time and tells me this is very important. Then he pricks a needle into a vein in my forearm. The needle is thicker than I'm used to from my previous recovery injections. The thickness is to minimize any damage to the red blood cells. Fuentes attaches the drip to the bag and opens the stopper. My arm begins to tingle as the cold blood seeps in, like goose pimples except they are inside my body. He retires to a chair by the desk.

Fifteen minutes later, when the bag has emptied into my arm, Fuentes gets to his feet. He unhooks the bag from the nail and tucks it away in his backpack with the needles and the drip. He puts on his coat, shakes my hand, and says, "Hasta luego." He leaves and I stay; my return flight doesn't leave till the following morning. I kick off my shoes and stare up at the ceiling. I'm cold and not exactly thrilled to be spending the night in a room where I have just done something that could cost me years of my career. I try to relax, but it's asking too much. At the end of a restless night of next to no sleep, I'm glad to see the sun rise. I skip breakfast and head straight to the airport for my flight back to Pisa.

The euphoria only hits me once I'm in the air. I've done it. I have given myself this gift. I can hardly wait to get back on my bike; I want to know how it feels. Every rider is curious about what it feels like to ride on dope, and my own curiosity could bump off a dozen cats. As soon as I reach home, I head out on my bike. I can feel the power in my legs even before I've left Lucca. I'm riding so smoothly, so easily that it scares me. I have to hold back so as not to take every climb at full tilt. I keep whispering to myself, "Easy now, easy."

The Tirreno starts on a Wednesday. The morning before the first stage, there's a doping check by the Union Cycliste Internationale (UCI), the sport's governing body. It tests my hematocrit. It's 44.5—no worries. My score is always there or thereabouts.

In the race itself I can feel how much I have left to give on every climb. I sail through the opening stages. My teammates can see that I'm in good shape, and the likes of Michael Boogerd, Óscar Freire, Juan Antonio Flecha, and Marc Wauters keep me out of the wind. During one particularly wet and windy stage, Wauters stays with me the whole day—even when I stop to take a leak. He fetches my rain jacket, helps me put it on when I get tangled up in it, and steers me through the peloton. It does me good to see a rider of Wauters's caliber sacrificing his own race for mine. I feel unbeatable. And no, guilt doesn't come into it. I tell myself that I'm not cheating, that everyone else is doing the same. I convince myself that I've only done what needs to be done to keep up with the big boys—nothing more, nothing less.

With two days to go till the end of the race, there's a time trial. Thirteen riders still have a chance of overall victory, and I am one of them. I ride a blistering stage and slaughter all of my rivals, taking third behind Fabian Cancellara and Leif Hoste. It's enough to give me the leader's jersey. On the days that follow, my teammates ride themselves into an early grave to get me to the finish. We're under attack until the bitter end, but no one gets away from us. In San Benedetto del Tronto, the finish of the final stage, I cross the line with my arms aloft. I've won the Tirreno, ahead of Jörg Jaksche and Alessandro Ballan. Jaksche later tells me he was riding on the strength of two blood bags he had banked the previous winter.

I am called to the podium and then to the press conference. I shake hands with sponsors and local dignitaries. My phone doesn't stop ringing. Reporters, family, friends. At the team dinner that evening we uncork one bottle of Champagne after another.

It's late in the evening by the time I open the door to my hotel room. I sit down on the bed and burst into tears. It all comes flooding out of me: the elation, the weeks of punishing training, but also the stress. The lonely months in an Italian hotel, the trips to Madrid, the secret I carry with me and can never divulge to anyone—it's all too much, and I'm back to being a boy of 21. Marc Wauters, my roommate, sits down beside me and puts his arm around my shoulders. I feel very small indeed.

15

ONE IS NOT ENOUGH

DON'T BELIEVE THEM, the riders who tell you they've tried doping but only once. Cross that line and there's no way back. Using a little dope is like being a tiny bit pregnant. Doping is addictive—not the stuff itself but the success it brings. I'm not addicted to blood bags, but I am addicted to the feeling of invincibility that flowed through my veins during the Tirreno–Adriatico.

In the weeks after the Tirreno, I make several more trips to Madrid. It's a logistical nightmare at times. Usually the team books all my flights, but I buy these tickets with my own credit card. I do it with a knot in my stomach, knowing the payments can be traced if Fuentes's network is ever busted. I have to time things to perfection. I fob the team off with some excuse to get out of riding the Critérium International; the race coincides with a transfusion appointment.

On March 19, 2006, I give a bag of blood in Madrid. Less than two weeks later it's reinfused, on March 30 to be precise, just ahead of the Tour of the Basque Country. Once again, the scene of the crime is the TRYP Hotel. The modus operandi is the same: disinfect arm, hang bag on nail, goose pimples inside my arm. When we're finished, Fuentes says to me, "Stay in this room." He makes it clear that he has a few other customers to attend to at the hotel that day, and he doesn't want us bumping into one another. Of course, all this does is arouse my curiosity. As soon as Fuentes leaves the room, I head for the balcony, where I have a good view of the hotel entrance. I see plenty of businessmen and vacationers but no one I recognize. Then, just as I'm about to step back inside, I spot a familiar face hurrying through the crowd, a young guy with blond hair. It's Remmert Wielinga, my teammate at Rabobank. A good time trialist, a good climber, and another rider managed by Jacques Hanegraaf.

A few days later, during the Tour of the Basque Country, I try to broach the subject with Remmert. He's a bit of an odd character, a good rider but not big on social skills. And I don't know him well enough to just drop the name Fuentes into the conversation. "And? In good shape?" I ask. "I mean, really, really good shape?" "Yes," he nods, "I'm in really good shape." "Good," I say, "me too." Perhaps unsurprisingly, he later denied any connection with Fuentes.

That one extra blood bag in my veins isn't enough to keep me up there with the best on the roads of the Basque Country. The pace is so ruthless, it cracks me at times. It's not like I haven't been warned; the peloton has dubbed the Basque Tour a "scooter race" because there are days when the Spaniards seem to be doing 50 kilometers per hour (kph) from start to finish without breaking a sweat. On one stage, I'm struggling my way up a mountain, lactic acid coming out of my ears, when Riccardo Riccò and Ángel Gómez Marchante stop to take a leak like they're out on a Sunday stroll. I draw my conclusion: If you want to be in the mix on the Basque Tour, you'd better take your dope to the next level.

After the spring classics, where I ride in the service of Boogerd and Freire to repay them for their efforts on my behalf at the Tirreno, I fly down to Madrid twice in quick succession to give blood—on April 26 and May 10. My aim is to build up a nice little stockpile in preparation for the Tour de France. These gifts to myself are to be stored away in the freezer.

The first date—April 26—is three days after Liège–Bastogne–Liège. I fly down to Madrid to find Fuentes waiting for me at the airport. We walk to his car. This time we skip the TRYP Hotel and head for an apartment somewhere in Madrid. He says it belongs to his parents and that they're away. The place doesn't exactly look lived in. As soon as we're through the door I take an envelope from my inside pocket. It contains €10,000, withdrawn from my account at the Rabobank in Tuitjenhorn a few days earlier. Fuentes makes a dismissive gesture. "No, no, later, later," he says. But I want rid of the dough, the sooner the better, and I shove the envelope into his hands. Not my smartest move in retrospect, but then I didn't know that the Spanish police had been hot on Fuentes's trail for months.

He sits me down in an old brown leather armchair and taps two bags of blood. Then he drives me back to the airport.

When I return to Madrid on May 10, it's not Fuentes but an assistant who is there to meet me. He introduces himself as Alberto Leon and explains that he'll be filling in for Fuentes this time around. He strikes me as a friendly young guy, and with the help of hand gestures galore we chat away in the car. His plan is to take me to a hotel to withdraw the blood, but it's conference season in Madrid, and we end up scouring the city in his little hatchback for hours without finding a vacancy. Eventually he gives up, and we drive out to his hometown, San Lorenzo de El Escorial, around 50 kilometers north of Madrid, where we check into a small hotel. Alberto taps a bag of blood and then makes himself scarce.

I go out in the evening for a bite to eat. Alone. I feel lost in this little town, and I can't call anyone because my SIM card has to stay out of my phone. I have a bad night's sleep in the hotel, and the next morning Alberto's brother turns up to give me a lift back to the airport. Stuck in the rush-hour traffic, I sit there next to a stranger in a business suit on his way to work in Madrid. As the car radio blares away in Spanish, I think about his life and mine. I try to imagine what it must be like to hop into your family sedan every day and brave the morning traffic jam for the sake of the old nine-to-five. It's beyond me.

Back home in Italy, I start a training block of a couple of weeks to get myself into shape for the Tour de France. Sometimes I train alone and sometimes I have company. Plenty of other riders live nearby, and I go out on regular training rides with Jörg Jaksche, who rides for Liberty Seguros. The more we ride together, the more we confide in each other. My eagerness to talk cracks him up sometimes. "Other riders are so difficult and secretive about it all," he laughs. "And here you are almost boasting about how much dope you use."

The Giro d'Italia comes to Lido di Camaiore that year, and we ride down together to soak up the atmosphere. After the race, we ride over to a hotel not far from the finish where Jörg's former team, CSC, is staying. We hang around the parking lot and shoot the breeze with a few people he knows. I look around and spot a little rental car pulling into one of the parking spaces. The driver gets out, shoulders a backpack, and strolls into the hotel without looking at anyone. It's Alberto Leon, Fuentes's assistant. On the way back home, Jörg tells me Alberto has a nickname: Ali Baba.

16
STEPPING UP

TUESDAY, MAY 23, 2006, A MEMORABLE EVENING. I'm sitting in a restaurant in Lucca having dinner with another cyclist who makes use of Fuentes's services. I won't mention his name—I suppose it's up to him to come clean. His phone rings. It's Jörg Jaksche on the line. He's in the middle of a team training camp, and he's not calling for a friendly chat. He has news, bad news. I see the face of the man across from me tighten. Then I watch him break down.

"They're on to him, Thomas," he says between sobs. "Fuentes has been arrested." His eyes dart all over the place, as if he's scared of being nabbed then and there. I'm not. All I can think about is the three bags of blood in that freezer and how I can get them back. It's only when I realize they must be in the hands of the Spanish police that I start cursing. All that effort, all that stress, all those clandestine flights these past few weeks—it's all been for nothing.

It's only when the anger and frustration have ebbed away that the fear takes hold. Fear that I might have been filmed or photographed. Fear that my name will turn up somewhere. My parents are visiting me in Lucca at the time. That evening I tell them my blood was in Fuentes's freezer when he was raided by the police. Mom clasps her hand to her mouth, Dad shakes his head solemnly. I call Jacques Hanegraaf. He tells me not to do anything. Sit tight and keep your mouth shut.

That's exactly what I do. I act like nothing's happened. Dad takes the prepaid phone I used to contact Fuentes and tosses it into the water at Viareggio. I try to focus on my training and fail miserably. In the days and weeks after the police raids, more and more details leak out. Rumors circulate, names emerge. The names of teams and riders. Jan Ullrich, Ivan Basso, a small peloton of Spaniards. Jörg Jaksche is also mentioned. Online and in the papers I see excerpts from the police dossier that is now widely known as Operation Puerto—documents that contain the number 24, along with the dates on which I gave blood. It turns out that Fuentes has given me a nickname: Clasicomano Luigi. To him I am Luigi Cecchini's classics guy. In a taped conversation with one of his accomplices, he refers to me as "the spy from the distant Italian."

Every moment of every day I find myself expecting a phone call with news that my name has surfaced. The uncertainty eats away at me. I toss and turn at night, sick to my stomach. I can barely focus on my cycling. At the start of June I have to compete in the

Dauphiné Libéré, but it's a lost cause from the start. I drag myself through the stages and can't even bring myself to talk to my fellow riders in the evenings.

Not being able to share my thoughts or fears with anyone takes its toll. I'm not good at bottling up my feelings. The team managers don't seem especially interested; nobody asks me what's wrong. At the national championships at the end of June, I put in another worthless performance. I have my blood tested at the lab in Amstelveen, and the results show that I'm anemic. No big surprise considering I've had three blood bags tapped, I've trained hard, and I'm being eaten up by stress. The team decides not to select me for the Tour de France. I accept the decision without a murmur of protest; if anything, it's a relief. Especially when even more names start to emerge in connection with Fuentes, and the Tour directors bar a number of riders and teams from lining up for the start. Only once the Tour is under way do I breathe more easily. Slowly but surely the focus shifts toward the doping scandals that come to light during the race itself.

It's around this time that I get to know Linda. She's a friend of my good friend Dirk Bellemakers, and we wind up having dinner with him one Friday evening at a restaurant in Bergeijk, on the Dutch-Belgian border. As soon as I set eyes on her, my cares evaporate. It's love at first sight. She is bright, blonde, and beautiful. I ask Dirk for her number and text her that same evening. In the days that follow we text back and forth, and the frequency increases. I have butterflies in my stomach every time my phone pings.

We arrange to go out for a meal. I pour on the charm, and I'm in luck: she's in love with me too. We kiss and start seeing each other regularly. One hot, sticky summer evening we make love for the first time. This is new to me—the first loving relationship in my life.

We see as much of each other as we can, in Holland and in Italy. During the cycling season she flies down on the weekends when I'm not racing. I pick her up at Pisa, and we go straight to McDonald's at the airport for ice cream. To begin with we stay at the apartment Stefano Cecchini shares with his girlfriend, and later I buy my own place in Lucca. For Linda these trips to Italy are mini-holidays. We sleep well into the morning, have breakfast at a local bar, stroll through the city, go shopping, head out to the beach. On Sunday evenings we have pizza at the Cecchinis' home. We talk for hours on end. It's all so natural, so innocent. Linda and I are just two young people in love. But for all her beauty, for all the good times we share, I still can't stay faithful to her. The temptation of other women is too strong. It's like my thirst for winning races: I always want more.

Little by little, the fear of being unmasked as one of Fuentes's customers begins to fade. The stress begins to ebb from my body. The whole episode could have been a warning, a lesson learned. But it isn't. My hunger for glory and my appetite for quick success win out over my fear of getting caught. If I learn anything it's that I'm still getting away with it. The notion that I am untouchable only grows stronger. And so the madness continues.

In August, after finishing ninth in the Eneco Tour, I decide to go in search of alternative means of doping. With my blood bags in the hands of the Spanish police, I opt for a less sophisticated approach. I want EPO. I ask the Rabobank team doctors, Geert Leinders and Jean-Paul van Mantgem. Van Mantgem says he's prepared to help me. He and I get along well—he's funny, he's smart, and he understands what makes me tick. Unlike Jacques Hanegraaf or Eufemiano Fuentes, he's not out to earn money by helping me dope; to him it's a way of controlling what I do. He knows I'll only look elsewhere if he turns me down. On a little white square of paper, he draws up a schedule for me in the lead-up to the Tour de Pologne: 2,000 units, every evening and every morning, five days in a row. One week before the race I have to stop using. And then three or four days before the race I have to take another single dose of 2,000 units.

I purchase the EPO across the German border, at a pharmacy called Barbarossa in Aachen. From teammates and training buddies I know they are not exactly sticklers for prescriptions. It's like buying my first pack of condoms; I take a deep breath, step inside, and ask for what I want as casually as possible. The woman behind the counter doesn't bat an eyelid, and I conclude that I am far from being their only EPO customer. I pay €400 in cash and leave with a set of ampoules and a couple of syringes. At home I tear open the packaging, fill a syringe with EPO, and inject it intravenously into my arm. I already know how to do this; by this stage I'm more or less a dab hand at hooking myself up to a recovery drip. I squeeze the syringe, and as its contents disappear into my bloodstream, it dawns on me that I have crossed another line. I feel nothing.

Before I travel to Poland, I have my blood checked. Van Mantgem arranges the appointment; it's at the Amstelveen hospital where he works when he's not working for the team. The check is a safety net, an added precaution to make sure that my blood levels are within the bounds. With a hematocrit above 50 in a random UCI test, I wouldn't even be allowed to start—a situation to be avoided at all costs. As it turns out, there is no cause for alarm; the check reveals a hematocrit of 48.3 and hemoglobin of 15.8. As agreed, I send a coded text message to Van Mantgem that my heart rate was 158 during the day's training session.

My blood values boosted by the injections, I expect to fly my way through the Tour de Pologne. And go flying I do. In the third stage, a dog runs out into the road directly in front of my wheel. I slam right into it, go head over heels, and stretch out my arms to break my fall. I feel the bones in my hand crack as I hit the ground.

Crash, bang, wallop. End of season.

17

A HIPPIE IN LOVE

WE'RE FLYING HIGH, so close to the sun it seems the wings might melt. I look out of the window and see nothing but ocean beneath us. Michael Boogerd is sitting next to me. We're on our way to Curaçao for an all-expenses-paid holiday, courtesy of Amstel Beer. I nudge Michael. I can't keep it to myself any longer. "You know all that hassle with Fuentes," I whisper. "I was one of his customers too." "Yeah? Oh, right," he replies, and takes another sip of his drink. He's not in the least bit surprised.

Michael and I have grown closer. We train together, drink together, frequent the same crummy bars during the training camps. We are lead riders for the same team. My contract with Rabobank is renewed and bumped up another level: in the 2007 and 2008 seasons, I stand to earn €800,000 a year—almost $1.3 million as the euro climbs to its all-time high. On the advice of

Jacques Hanegraaf I move to Monaco, where "tax" is a dirty word. I share an apartment with Australian sprinter Baden Cooke, but I'm hardly ever there.

The 2007 season is my third as a pro. Within the team I've long since outgrown the status of rising young talent, not least because that's no longer how I see myself. The team and I share the same expectations: Thomas Dekker is in it to win it.

In February we take part in the Vuelta a Mallorca, which is preceded by a training camp. Six days before we're due to race, I go into a pharmacy with teammate Max van Heeswijk and buy testosterone patches. On his advice I cut the patches open and rub the gel onto my skin so that it will be absorbed better. The evening before the race we both use GHB, the date-rape drug. Max has brought some with him in a couple of miniature shampoo bottles, the kind you find in hotel rooms. After dinner, we mix the GHB with a little soft drink and swallow it down. Once it kicks in, I float around the hotel for a while like a hippie in love, feeling out of this world. The moment I flop onto my bed I'm out for the count.

I wake up the next morning fully dressed. I rub my eyes, drag myself to the bathroom, and pull on my cycling gear. A few hours later I'm crossing the finish line with my hands held high: I win the most prestigious stage of the Vuelta a Mallorca. I'm over the moon till it dawns on me that the winner has to undergo a dope check. I know that testosterone is traceable for five days and GHB for only four hours, but just to be sure I empty my bladder at the side of the road before heading over for my inspection. That way it will take a little longer before they have a sample of my urine for testing. In the end the doping officer has to come back to the hotel with me; it's hours before I can take another piss. I hear nothing more about it.

The months that follow are anything but smooth sailing. Ahead of the Tour of the Basque Country I buy a new supply of EPO—under the counter—at a pharmacy just outside Lucca. It doesn't have any effect. Through Van Mantgem I have bought a device to test my own hematocrit. Most of the team's top riders have one. The reading shows no increase, despite the EPO. It happens sometimes. Your body is not a machine; it doesn't always respond the way you want it to. When I tell Michael Boogerd, he laughs long and loud.

As if that wasn't enough, my hip starts playing up during the Basque Tour. There's some kind of friction in the socket, and it hurts, especially when I'm tucked low with my hands on the drops. For weeks on end, my hip has to be loosened up by a soigneur almost every day. The silver lining to this cloud is that we don't have to invent any excuses for using cortisone; for once I can obtain a doctor's note for a genuine problem. In the course of the spring classics I receive a number of cortisone shots from the team doctors. Every doctor's note is documented in a medical booklet that I have to take along to all my doping checks. In the waiting room I sometimes take a look at other riders' booklets. Thick as Bibles, some of them.

It's only in Switzerland's Tour de Romandie, at the start of May, that I begin to get into my racing. Maybe the EPO from two weeks earlier is finally kicking in, or maybe I'm just hitting a streak of good form. The weather is lousy the entire week, but that doesn't trouble me. In the penultimate mountain stage I finish second behind Igor Antón. And I win the final time trial, and with it the general classification, ahead of Paolo Savoldelli, Andrey Kashechkin, Cadel Evans, and Chris Horner. This is different from my victory in the Tirreno–Adriatico. That was a breakthrough, while this is merely confirmation, a stepping-stone on my way to a higher goal. That goal is the Tour de France. I don't even take the time to savor my victory in Romandie, though Kees, Karien, and Linda are there to see it. As soon as it's over, the four of us drive from Switzerland back to Luyksgestel at 220 kph through the night. I deal with the speeding fines later.

The road to the Tour de France leads through the Tour de Luxembourg, the Tour de Suisse, and the national championships. But my hip is refusing to cooperate. I have to scratch Luxembourg altogether, and I'm in so much pain on the longer training rides that my expectations of the Tour de Suisse couldn't be lower. I treat myself to a couple of shots of EPO, if only to give myself a glimmer of hope.

The day before I leave for Switzerland, I have a night out in Lucca with Tyler Hamilton, who lives only a few streets away. He is one of the nicest guys I know in the world of cycling—warm, friendly, and not afraid to show his softer side. But that evening he's in a bad way. He has a doping ban behind him, and ever since he's been struggling to recover his old form. Mentally, he has taken some hard knocks. He's trained for months for the Giro d'Italia, only to have his team—Tinkoff—drop him from the race. We drink wine that evening, way too much wine. Tyler talks about his time at U.S. Postal. About Lance. About Lance's medical guru, Michele Ferrari. About blood doping. About the world of lies of which I too am a part. Our night out ends at sunrise, and Tyler drives me to the airport.

In the Tour de Suisse, my morale is low, and it shows during the opening stages. But a couple of days in, things start to look up. On stage 5, a truncated mountain stage to the ski resort of Crans-Montana, my teammate Jan Boven takes me to the front ahead of the final climb. To be honest, I wish he hadn't; his efforts mean I can't allow myself to lose touch at the first signs of acceleration. So I hang on. Part of me is thinking, "I'll drop back in a little while. Maybe with 5 kilometers to go, and otherwise at the four-k sign." But 4 kilometers comes and goes, and I'm still hanging in there. So does 3. With 2 kilometers left, I decide to throw in the towel when we see the flamme rouge, the "one-more-to-go" red pennant. But when we pass under it, there are only a few riders left. At a traffic island I spot the chance for a break. I put a spurt on and lurch my way through the next 200 meters with my tongue hanging out. When I look round, the rest are nowhere to be seen. I glide across the line like an albatross—arms stretched wide. Jan Boven finishes as I'm standing on the podium. I wave at him and shout, "Hey, Jan! Look who won!" He shakes his head in disbelief.

On the second-to-last day of the Tour de Suisse there's a doping test. My hematocrit is 41.5. Not high at all. But there's another problem: The quantity of newly formed red blood cells in my blood is on the low side, an effect of the EPO shots I gave myself. They end up stalling the body's natural production of new red blood cells after a while. This could be a reason for the UCI to keep tabs on me. I'm thoroughly pissed off about it, but the thought of changing my ways never crosses my mind.

The peloton is rife with rumors that there's a new EPO product on the market. Dynepo is the name—more effective than ordinary EPO and more difficult to trace because it stimulates the production of red blood cells through the body's own protein hormone. I discuss Dynepo with Michael Boogerd, who takes an interest. He checks into it and soon establishes a connection, through a Slovenian athlete by the name of Boštjan Buč. Michael invests in a supply, which is sent to his house in a refrigerated truck. In turn, I tap into Michael's stockpile. I take two shots of 8,000 units on the Monday and Tuesday after the national championships.

I'm all set. Bring on the Tour.

18

THE 2007 TOUR DE FRANCE

MY FIRST TOUR DE FRANCE is Michael Boogerd's last. It turns out to be my last too, but at the time it seems like the first of many. We share a room. Ten years ago I sat cheering on Michael in front of the TV at our vacation campsite, and now here I am, in the Tour and roommates with my boyhood idol for the next three weeks.

We chat away nonstop. Michael tells me he's been blood doping for the past few years. First through a Vienna clinic called Humanplasma—our teammates Michael Rasmussen and Denis Menchov were customers there too—and when that network was rounded up, the two Michaels joined forces with an Austrian sports agent by the name of Stefan Matschiner. It wasn't much of a leap for Matschiner: He simply bought up what was left of the Humanplasma operation, took a course in how to give injections, and was good to go.

To my knowledge, Michael Boogerd does not use blood transfusions on the 2007 Tour. We're both on that form of EPO called
Dynepo from Slovenia. Michael and I inject 2,000 units eight times
during the Tour. I have no worries about getting caught; Michael
assures me Dynepo is untraceable, and I believe him. We also inject
cortisone every other day, a product called Diprofos. We have a
doctor's note for those shots, though I couldn't tell you what the
pretext was if you paid me. The whole exemption system is a sham.
In addition to helping us dig deeper during a race, cortisone keeps
us nice and skinny; my 6-foot 2-inch frame is carrying 150 pounds.
I've never been so lean in my life.

The Tour starts in London that year. We arrive almost a week
in advance, and on the Thursday before the start, the UCI carries
out drug tests. My hematocrit is 45, but Michael's is 50—teetering
on the very edge of what's permissible. All of a sudden he's a risk;
one point higher and he'll fail his doping test. The team doctors,
Leinders and Van Mantgem, suggest he hook himself up to a saline
drip every morning at six before the controllers come knocking,
the aim being to nudge his hematocrit down a notch or three.
"Good plan," says Michael.

That same evening we're sitting in our room, bored senseless.
We've cracked open a bottle of wine, but it's going to take more
than that to put a smile on our faces. Booze is fine, but girls are
finer. No sooner said than done: I go online to hook us up with a
couple of escorts, and at 1:00 a.m. a couple of Eastern European
hookers arrive at the door to our room. Michael and I are a little

disappointed; they both looked a good bit more appetizing in their web photos. It's not exactly the most glamorous rendezvous of all time, sneaking around in the middle of the night in our poky hotel room, but we make the best of it and finally get to sleep around three. Three hours later the alarm goes off. Michael has to get an IV bag of fluid into his system. For the first few days Van Mantgem hooks Michael up to the drip; after that he says he can do it himself. The alarm wakes me up at first, but after a few days I get used to it. At 6:00 a.m. Michael gets up to stick an IV drip in his arm, and I roll over and go back to sleep. If there's such a thing as a normal life, we're about as far removed from it as you can get.

In the 2007 Tour, we have one of the best teams in the entire peloton. In addition to Boogerd, I'm lining up alongside Michael Rasmussen, Denis Menchov, Óscar Freire, Pieter Weening, Juan Antonio Flecha, Grischa Niermann, and Bram de Groot. At the team meeting before the start, Rasmussen declares that he wants to win the Tour. That raises a smirk or two. I think he's full of shit, that he's saying whatever it takes to avoid working his ass off for anyone else. At this point none of us know that he's lied about his whereabouts or that he's doped up to the eyeballs—though we have our suspicions. Nor do we know that Leinders and Van Mantgem have been slipping him shots of Dynepo from my and Boogerd's supply; that only comes to light long after the Tour is over.

Rasmussen is skin and bone; you can look right through him. A rice cracker with nothing on it is all I ever see him eat. During one of the first flat stages, he's behind me when the peloton is put in the gutter. He calls on me to swing out into the middle of the road and shelter him so he can conserve energy. I think he's being an arrogant jerk, and I toy with the idea of telling him to go fuck himself. But since I'm pedaling away without a care in the world, I do what I can for him.

It soon becomes clear that Rasmussen's not bluffing; he's in the form of his life. In the first full-on mountain stage of the Tour, he launches his attack 60 kilometers from the finish. He shoots off like a comet, and we don't see him again till the finish in Tignes, wearing the yellow jersey. That evening at dinner, the mood is jubilant. It's Champagne all round—though the man of the hour takes only a sip or two—and the team managers keep the bottles coming. From that day on, we all ride for Rasmussen. He holds his own in the time trial, and in the mountain stages that follow he builds more of a lead over his main rivals, Alberto Contador, Cadel Evans, and Carlos Sastre. We actually start to believe that our crazy Dane can win the Tour.

Riders from other teams are caught for doping; Alexandre Vinokourov and Cristian Moreni are booted out the back door. But in our little Rabobank bubble, there's no talk of doping at all. Not even when stories start to surface in the media that Rasmussen lied when he said he was in Mexico before the Tour. We ask him no questions. If anything, there's a hush of respect. Boogerd and I agree that Rasmussen has been smart as hell. He's found himself a system, and it's clearly one that works. He's riding in the yellow jersey, for Christ's sake—what more proof do you want? Doping is everywhere. In our team, in the other teams. Dynepo, cortisone, blood bags, sleeping pills, early morning IV drips to keep our hematocrit down—when there's nothing but madness all around, it starts to seem normal after a while.

The final mountain stage that year takes us to the summit of the Aubisque. It's the most important day of the Tour, and we have to make sure Rasmussen comes away from the Pyrenees with his lead intact. Things get off to a strange start. The air is thick with doping rumors. Rasmussen's in the firing line, the Astana team has pulled out, and a couple of the French and German teams strike in protest, insisting they've had enough of doping cheats killing their sport. I remain cool and focused, thinking only about the race ahead.

The stage unfolds calmly enough, but the more cols we pass, the more we come under attack. We have to give everything, yet I'm riding so smooth and easy that I hardly feel my legs. That day I'm a team in my own right. I ride up and down the mountains with my head in the wind, charge through the valleys. On my wheel, the peloton soon stretches into a very thin line. Now and then Rasmussen yells at me not to get too carried away. It's my best day ever on a bike.

Before the final climb I give way. I can see in Rasmussen's face that he's still fresh as tomorrow's headlines, and even before the stage reaches its climax, I know. We've done it. The Tour is ours. The mood on the bus is nothing short of euphoric. It's high fives all round, the air is buzzing with talk of how we'll celebrate in Paris. But before we even make it back to the hotel, the atmosphere changes. Theo de Rooij receives a phone call. His face darkens, and he stalks off to the shower area so no one can listen in.

I have no idea what's going on, but the penny begins to drop when I get a call from Stefano Cecchini. He tells me Enrico Cassani, who's commentating for Italian TV, claims he bumped into Rasmussen in the Dolomites when according to his official whereabouts he should have been in Mexico. This is not good news. By the time the bus pulls up outside the hotel in Pau, our elation has dissolved.

Boogerd and I still don't see how this Mexico scandal could have major consequences. Until there's a knock on the door. It's Rasmussen. As soon as he walks into our room, I can tell he's been crying. "I'm out of the Tour," he says. "What?" Boogerd exclaims. "What do you mean?" "It's Theo," Rasmussen stammers. "Theo's taking me out of the Tour." I leap up from my bed. Boogerd is fuming; so am I. We try to reassure Rasmussen, tell him we'll have a word with Theo de Rooij, sort this thing out.

We storm down the hall in search of De Rooij and find him in his room. As soon as we're in the door, we let fly. "What the hell is going on? Taking Rasmussen out of the Tour? Are you out of your mind?" We can scream, plead, and beg all we like; De Rooij is an immovable object. "He has to go." The decision is final. Rasmussen will not start the next morning.

The pair of us are furious. It feels like we've been robbed. Shafted. I've been riding myself into the ground for nothing. It's not about losing out on the winners' bonus, it's about the honor of the

Tour victory we've been riding for as a team. That's all I can think of at that moment; all sense of reality has gone. I'm in a cocoon where different rules apply, a different moral code. Rasmussen lied, so what? Haven't we all bent the rules? The team doctors are helping us with our dope, for Christ's sake! I have never discussed doping with De Rooij, but I can't imagine for one second he thinks Rasmussen was about to win the Tour dope-free. The man wasn't born yesterday. At best, it looks to me as if the policy he and Erik Breukink are pursuing is one of turning a blind eye. They demand that we perform at the very highest level, but they don't need to know how. It seems asking no questions means never having to face the inconvenient truth.

Late that evening, there's a meeting on the team bus. We haven't a hope of speaking our minds in the hotel; the place is already crawling with reporters. The mood in the team is one I only know from funerals. A mix of rage, sorrow, and frustration. We make a unanimous decision not to start the next day, and it's agreed that a plane will fly in from Holland to pick us up. The spell is broken. I've had it. The weariness of the Tour washes over me. I'm not even hungry; that evening I eat nothing. Instead the whole team starts drinking.

Boogerd and I collapse onto our beds at four in the morning. Wiped out, all cycled out. But three hours later we wake to the sound of Erik Breukink banging on the door, telling us we have to start after all, that we can't simply walk away from the biggest race of the year. The future of the team is hanging in the balance, and the bank is insisting that we ride on. I have two words for him: "No way." Yet, to my amazement, Michael doesn't take much persuading. I stamp into the bathroom, slam the door behind me, and lie in the bath, letting the cold water splash over me. They can all go to hell. There's no fucking way I am turning up at that starting line. After 15 minutes or so, Piet, the driver of the team bus, comes up and sits with me. He pats me on the head, says he understands it's the last thing I want to do, but that getting back on my bike is still the best option. "If you won't do it for yourself, then do it for the team. For all of us." I sigh and heave myself out of the bath.

With over an hour to go before the stage kicks off, I am ready and waiting in the team bus. I stare out through the window with tears in my eyes. This was not how I thought my first Tour de France would end. When we get off the bus at the start, the crowd boos and hurls insults. *"Dopage!" "Tricheurs!"* Michael nearly punches a guy in the crowd who yells some insult in Dutch about doping.

I drag myself through the final four days to Paris. A massive party had been planned, complete with a yellow train to take us back to Rabobank headquarters in Utrecht. Instead, we gather in a nondescript room in some faceless Paris hotel. There is nothing to celebrate. That same evening, Kees, Karien, and Linda drive over to pick me up.

In the weeks, months, and years that follow, there is no evaluation of that Tour. It's as if no one wants to lift the lid on what happened in that team. No one asks us anything. Not De Rooij, not Breukink, not the bank. It all remains unspoken.

19

IT'S YOU, NOT ME

I CAN'T SEE IT. Maybe I don't want to see it. I'm heading straight for the abyss, but there's no slamming on the brakes. I'm well on the way to destroying my own career. I finish fourth in the Eneco Tour, win two stages and the general classification in the Hessen-Rundfahrt—but it's not enough. I want more, a bigger kick, a sharper edge. In the final months of his career, under the motto "everything must go," Michael Boogerd puts his foot on the doping accelerator, and I'm not about to be left behind. Ahead of the world championships in Stuttgart, we train together and inject the last of his Dynepo supply. I transfer a few grand to his account to cover my share.

Michael and I are roommates in Stuttgart. I break every speed limit getting there, roaring down the highway in my brand-new Porsche 911. We test our hematocrit a few days before the race,

and we're both sky high, so on the morning of the world championships we set the alarm for 6:00 to get an IV bag of fluid into our
systems. The controllers turn up right on cue one hour later, and
there doesn't appear to be any problem. I ride a jet-propelled race,
covering every single break and finishing just outside the top 10.
But after the race I have to take another drug test. This is strange—
I've never been tested twice in a single day before.

Dion van Bommel, one of Rabobank's team doctors, goes with
me to the test. "Thomas," he sighs, "this morning your fucking
hematocrit was 49.6." This comes as a shock. I expected it to be
high but not to be pushing 50, especially with a bag of saline solution in my veins. The UCI has called me in for a second check
because I'm suspect.

That evening I get a call from Jean-Paul van Mantgem. He is
seething. The reason the team doctors keep an eye on my doping is to make sure I don't take it too far and attract unwelcome
scrutiny from the UCI. The team orders me to report to the lab
in Amstelveen the next morning for an additional blood test. And
they pull me out of the Circuit Franco-Belge in case I end up being
tested again by the UCI. "It's a risk we're not prepared to take,"
Van Mantgem says.

It's the first time the team has reined me in. Doping is not the
problem; it's running the risk of getting caught. I can use all the cortisone, blood bags, and EPO I like, as long as I don't bring the team
into discredit. And of course Rabobank has become 10 times touch-
ier since the whole Rasmussen affair. All I can see is the hypocrisy.

I feel like they're trying to put me down. It strikes me as a bit rich that the same doctor who is drawing up EPO schedules for me is now telling me to ease back on the throttle.

After the 2007 season, the team is swept clean. Rabobank has been swamped by a shitload of negative publicity, and the managing directors are terrified of being caught up in another doping scandal. The bankers never dreamed of interfering with the running of the team before, but times have clearly changed. Where once they were content to chuck a bag of money over the fence, now they are determined to keep their finger on the pulse.

Theo de Rooij is sent packing as team director. He is to be replaced by a man from the bank, Harold Knebel. Rasmussen has been fired, and Boogerd has retired. The whereabouts system is tightened up to enable doping control officers to track down riders wherever they may be. And the UCI introduces the biological passport, a means of keeping better track of the fluctuations in riders' blood values.

The team changes, cycling changes. Thomas Dekker stays the same. With the season at an end, I go out for a night on the town with a few teammates, including Michael Boogerd. It is the evening of the Cycling Gala in Den Bosch—a glitzy annual event where the winner of Cyclist of the Year is announced—but we end up at the door of Yab Yum, Amsterdam's most infamous brothel. I drink and fuck all night.

The sun has long since come up by the time the €3,500 bill is settled and we stagger out into the daylight. The morning paper has already hit the doormat. Michael Boogerd picks it up, flicks through to the sports pages, and I see that I haven't been crowned Cyclist of the Year. I can't help but feel pissed; I had 10 victories to my name in 2007, but apparently it's not enough. I need more. That's all well and good, but Michael's Dynepo supply has run out, and the stuff's not easy to get hold of. So I ask Michael for Stefan Matschiner's number.

I call Matschiner toward the end of the year. It's a short conversation. I ask him if he has room for new customers, and his answer is yes. In mid-December, we meet for the first time in a small conference room at the Hilton at Schiphol Airport. He is a different breed from Fuentes, a good bit younger—early thirties at a guess—and he has a lot more to say for himself. With his jacket, jeans, and expensive taste in shoes, he could easily be in the running for Young Businessman of the Year, if his business wasn't doping.

Like Fuentes, he offers a long-term and a short-term system for blood transfusion. I can also get my hands on Dynepo through him. He launches into a spiel about the benefits and drawbacks of the various types of doping, but I know all the details and I know what I want. I am still only 23 but wise beyond my years. I take charge of the conversation. I tell Matschiner I want blood doping on the long-term system and that I want two bags tapped by Christmas. "No problem," he replies. Then he starts talking money. His fee is a cool €15,000 a year—about $22,000 at the time—plus 10 percent of my winnings. He suggests sending me invoices for training consultation, but I'm not having it. "Cash only," I tell him and insist that from now on I will only contact him on a prepaid phone. Matschiner agrees, and we part with the words "See you soon."

On December 23, 2007, I fly to Austria from Brussels and arrange to meet Jacques Hanegraaf early in the morning at Zaventem Airport to tell him what I'm up to. Our relationship is still so close that I want him to be part of this. Jacques gives his blessing to my Matschiner deal, pleased that I've found a new deep freeze for my blood bags. "Nice job" is his verdict.

On the plane to Austria, I'm surrounded by winter vacationers, chatting away about pistes, ski lifts, and powdery snow. Matschiner meets me at the airport and drives me to a little village called Steyrermühl, pulling up in front of an insurance office with a big sign outside that says UNIQA. We walk into what looks like any other office: desks, computers, and shelves crammed with files. But once we are in the basement, I spot a blood centrifuge in among the filing cabinets and boxes of brochures. Next to it is a big fridge. I sit down in an armchair. Matschiner pricks a needle into a vein in my forearm and connects a drip to an empty bag. I give two bags of blood, almost a liter in total. Matschiner dates them and pops them in the freezer. He follows that up with two shots of Dynepo to stimulate the production of red blood cells. Then we leave. On our way back to the airport, Matschiner takes a detour past the house he's building. "What can I say? Business is booming." That same evening I wing my way back to Brussels.

I spend that night at Linda's and wake up the next morning at around 10:30 to see that I have 11 missed calls, all from my dad.

I call him back right away. He talks fast. "There's a doping officer on Kees's doorstep. They're trying to find you." Holy shit. I remember putting "Luyksgestel" on my whereabouts form. I pull on my shirt and trousers, jump into the Porsche, and hightail it to Kees and Karien's place, around 10 kilometers away. I'm in luck; even though I've kept him hanging around for hours, the doping controller is still there. I mumble an apology, pee in a container, seal it, and sign the papers. As the controller is leaving, I slip him a bottle of wine for his trouble.

I can still see him heading off down the garden path with the cooler in his hand, my sample inside. I know it's not been long since those two shots of Dynepo, but I have no fear of discovery. There's no way they can trace it.

Not then they can't.

20

TRICKIER THAN YOU'D THINK

THERE'S A POOL OF BLOOD ON THE BATHROOM FLOOR, and I am sitting in it. I stick the thick needle in my arm. Again and again and again. It won't stay put. It won't fucking stay put. I thought I'd be able to do this job myself, empty a bag of blood into my veins, but it's trickier than I thought. The needle is thicker than I'm used to, and I can't get the fucking thing into a vein. My arm is turning into a pincushion. It's four in the morning, and I'm so tired I can hardly see straight. I curse myself. I curse that jerkoff Matschiner and the clueless sidekick he sent to deliver the blood bag to my apartment in Lucca. Why couldn't he have sent someone who actually knows how to hook up a drip?

I'm over the edge. I've crossed every line. I'm using blood bags, injecting Dynepo, asking the team for cortisone shots. If this is poker, I'm all in. The team no longer has a hold on me. At the first training camp in Spain I meet the Rabobank team's new director, Harold Knebel. For a banker he's a nice guy, but he knows zip about cycling. He has no idea what's going on in the team, past or present.

I keep my mouth shut with Knebel, but I do confide in Jean-Paul van Mantgem about my latest blood doping connection. He seems happy; by using blood bags, I run the least risk of getting caught. "But," he adds immediately, "we have to make sure your hematocrit is no higher than 45 percent, 46 tops. Otherwise your blood profile will attract attention." I nod, but his words go straight through my head, in one ear and out the other.

At the start of 2008, I'm still having hip trouble, and I start to fall behind with my training. The cavalry comes in the shape of Brabant-based masseur Cor van Wanroy. Under his expert care my hip improves. Ahead of the Vuelta a Castilla y León I use a few shots of Dynepo—signed, sealed, and delivered to me by DHL courtesy of Michael Boogerd's Slovenian connection. Michael pays the Slovenian, and I pay Michael. On Dynepo and with my hip fixed, I sail through my races and end up third overall in Castilla y León, finishing top three in just about every stage.

For the Tour of the Basque Country I want to chuck a blood bag into the mix. Matschiner was supposed to deliver it in person, but something must have come up. Instead, a pal of his brings it to my door in Lucca in the middle of the night. He doesn't have the know-how to take care of the transfusion, and besides, he's in a hurry. He has to rush on to Rome with a car full of dope for a bunch of Italian athletes.

So here I am with my own blood all over the bathroom floor. Somewhere in the back of my mind a voice is screaming at me to throw the bag away, to finally start thinking clearly about what the hell I'm doing. But I refuse to listen. I will get that blood into my veins. I have to. And thank Christ, I manage it at last. Shortly before six, as the day begins to dawn, the blood is where it should be—pumping through my body. I rinse out the empty bag, cut it into pieces, and throw it in the garbage.

In the Tour of the Basque Country, I finish third in the general classification behind Alberto Contador and Cadel Evans. I fly back to Holland and head for Kees and Karien's place in Luyksgestel, where Matschiner is due to arrive to give me another blood bag as a boost ahead of the spring classics. It's as if he's delivering pizza. At home he packs a blood bag into his suitcase, flies to Dusseldorf, rents a car, and drives to my home away from home. He takes a painting off the bedroom wall, hangs the bag on the nail, hooks me up, and watches the blood flow into my veins. I pay him €15,000 in cash, and off he goes.

I feel invincible, untouchable, and I tell anyone who will listen that I am going to ride like a rocket in the spring classics. In an interview with Dutch TV, I assure the crew that they will be able to count the guys that finish ahead of me in the Amstel Gold Race on the fingers of one hand.

My blood is in great shape. One day before the race, a woman from the lab in Amstelveen comes to the hotel in Maastricht where the team is staying. Her test reveals that my hematocrit is 48.2, high enough to arouse the UCI's suspicions if they check me. I'm not the least bit worried, feeling fully prepped and happy as Larry. The same cannot be said of the team. The doctors go ballistic again, and it starts to dawn on them that I'm a loose cannon. The monster they have helped create is no longer theirs to control. They penalize me, tell me I'll have to ride the spring classics without a single cortisone injection, insisting that a doctor's note for a fake injury might make the UCI even more suspicious. To me, it's a ridiculous sanction. I whine and I wheedle to get cortisone from Van Mantgem and Van Bommel, but they don't give an inch.

The team doctors are also refusing to help me manage my hematocrit. On the morning of the Amstel Gold Race, I have to get a bag of fluid into my system all by myself. That's okay; I've already bought a couple of IV bags of saline at the pharmacy.

My roommate is Laurens ten Dam. I've known him for years. We both started cycling at the same little club in northern Holland. Laurens is one of the few riders I can vouch for with my hand on my heart: He is clean as a new whistle. He says doping just isn't his style. He rides for the fun of it and has gradually improved his performance over the years. He doesn't feel under any pressure to win the major races. Not from the team and not from within.

When the alarm goes off at 6:00, I get up as quietly as possible so as not to wake Laurens and set up a drip for myself in the bathroom. But I make a complete mess of it again. I jab the needle in my arm repeatedly, blood shooting everywhere. I look up to see Laurens peer sleepily around the bathroom door and then jump as he gets the shock of his life. By this time, there's blood spattered on the walls. When I finally manage to get my act together and the solution into my bloodstream, Laurens helps me clean the place up, shaking his head all the while.

My televised prediction comes true: One hand is all you need to count the guys who beat me. I finish fifth in the Amstel Gold Race, six seconds behind the winner, Damiano Cunego. Then it's off to Belgium and fifth place in La Flèche Wallonne road race, where Kim Kirchen wins, followed by sixth in Liège–Bastogne–Liège, behind Alejandro Valverde. I'm up there with the biggest names in cycling, but I'm riding on a cocktail of dope, stress, and insane ambition, way beyond the team's limits and my own.

Back in Switzerland at the Tour de Romandie, something inside snaps from one moment to the next. With one more mountain stage to go, I'm in the runner-up spot. The fact that I've got a bad case of the shits and I've been throwing up all night makes no difference. This race is mine. The next day I let the team work their butts off for me, determined to launch an attack on Andreas Klöden, the man ahead of me in the classification. But then as quickly as one pedal stroke leads to the next, I feel the strength drain from my legs. I know I'm done for, and I can't find the will to go on. I start coasting and slide out of the leading group. A TV motorbike comes and rides alongside me. I smile for the camera as if I don't have a care in the world. A few kilometers on I see the team bus parked at the feed zone. I get off my bike and climb aboard.

Everyone in the team is fuming, and the next morning I'm put on a train home. A soigneur drops me at a railway station somewhere in the middle of Switzerland, and that's that. I receive a phone call from Harold Knebel, who just about takes my head off. How could I let the whole team ride for me and then drop out just like that? It's unheard of. All I can do is laugh. The team has sent me from race to race, wrung me out like a wet sponge, and when I reach the breaking point suddenly I'm the scum of the earth? More to the point, what makes a banker think he can tell me how to ride my race? How would he like me telling him how to manage his interest rates?

I'm living in a dreamworld. I do what I please, preoccupied with myself and nothing else. I have enlisted the services of two young business managers, Eelco and Martijn Berkhout, to set up a cycling tour that bears my name: the Gran Fondo Thomas Dekker. The proceeds are to go to the Johan Cruyff Foundation, a charitable organization for children established by the legendary Dutch footballer and coach. To finalize the details, a meeting has been set up at the Olympic Stadium in Amsterdam. Johan Cruyff has flown in specially. His assistants are there, Martijn and Eelco are there. All waiting for me. Fifteen minutes go by. Thirty minutes. An hour. They call and call, but there's no answer. At last they get hold of me, two hours later when I wake up in my apartment in Lucca. The meeting with Cruyff had completely slipped my mind. Martijn and Eelco brazen it out, tell the great man it's because I'm training so hard and I've got way too much on my mind. Cruyff understands. "Logical" is his only comment.

The cracks in my relationship with Rabobank turn into fissures. I couldn't care less. If Rabobank isn't willing to back me, I'll find myself another team. Two weeks after the Tour de Romandie, I drive from Italy to Austria so that Matschiner can fill two blood bags in readiness for the Tour de France. On my way I drop in at a casino in the Slovenian town of Nova Gorica and blow a couple grand. Driving back home, I race over the Austrian autobahn at 200 kph—until the police catch up with me and spoil my fun. When I notice that one of the cops is wearing a watch that doubles as a heart-rate monitor, I turn on the charm and the sporting banter. I get off lightly—two €35 fines—and I laugh out loud as I zoom off down the highway. It's like I've morphed into The Joker from the Batman movies, so far gone that I genuinely believe I'm above the law, that I can get away with anything. I have success, money, women. I've been lionized by the public and the media. The world is at my feet. I'm climbing higher and higher. I've spread my wings, and here I am, soaring above everything and everyone.

But in reality, the descent has already begun.

At the end of May I get a phone call from Jean-Paul van Mantgem. There's a problem. The UCI has informed the team that the blood values in my biological passport are all over the place. They suspect me of doping, and I have been summoned to Switzerland, to UCI headquarters in Aigle. I can feel the blood drain from my face. This is a reality check if ever there was one. For months, years even, I've never had to justify myself to anyone, and now I have to explain to the powers that be why my blood values are bouncing up and down like a hyperactive kid in a candy store.

In the weeks that follow, I can't put in a decent training session. All my morale is gone. I've gone from cyclist to suspect. Jacques Hanegraaf has arranged legal counsel for me, a lawyer by the name of Hans van Oijen. We fly to Switzerland, where we are joined by Jean-Paul van Mantgem. He barely says a word to me.

Our appointment with the UCI is in a hotel conference room near Aigle, and the UCI is represented by Mario Zorzoli, an Italian doctor on the organization's medical committee. You could cut the tension with a knife. Zorzoli produces a document with my test results and explains how the system works.

"We take a rider's blood tests and feed them into a formula," Zorzoli begins. "The resulting percentage expresses the likelihood that the rider has been doping." He is silent for a moment. "In your case, that figure is 99.9 percent." His eyes meet mine. I say nothing. I have no idea what I should say.

My lawyer intervenes. "Yes, but there's a difference between 99.9 percent and 100 percent, right?"

"Uh . . . yes, that is correct," Zorzoli replies.

"So as long as that figure is not 100 percent, then my client is still allowed to race. Am I right?" Zorzoli nods.

Van Oijen produces a document from his attaché case. "In that case, would you be so kind as to confirm that fact, on behalf of the UCI? The fact that Thomas is allowed to race?" Van Oijen slides pen and paper across the table. Zorzoli sits back and scratches his head for a moment. Then he picks up the pen and signs. Van Oijen looks on contentedly.

To this day I have no idea why I was summoned to Switzerland. It's as if Zorzoli wants to warn me. As if he wants to let me know that the UCI has me in its sights. But what does he want to achieve? Does he want me to stop doping? Or to find better ways to cover my tracks?

Back at Rabobank, they're sick of me, and it shows. I am not selected for the Tour de France, nor do I get the nod to join the lineup for the national championships. I call their bluff and go anyway. I drive to Ootmarsum and check in at the team's hotel, but I'm given a room in a separate wing and excluded from everything. It's only by asking a couple of fellow riders that I find out where the team meeting is being held. When I run into Knebel and Breukink in the corridor, they stare me down, poker-faced. I grin back like a schoolboy who's just been sent out of the classroom. To show them they can't hurt me, I act tougher and cockier than I am.

When the real Tour begins, Rabobank packs me off to the Sachsen Tour, where I go through the motions. TV personality Wilfried de Jong does an item about me for his sports program, but even that leaves me cold. While the crew films the team coasting to the start of the next stage, I stop off to have a gander at a jeweler's window display. The camera keeps rolling while I ogle a bunch of overpriced watches. I'm a spoiled brat with delusions of grandeur, and I'm not ashamed to show it. At least, that's the impression I give. Arrogance becomes a suit of armor to keep everything and everyone at bay.

At the end of July, Dutch daily *de Volkskrant* reports that the UCI is keeping a close watch on me due to the fluctuations in my blood values. To this day I have no idea how they got hold of the story. I shrug it off and act like the whole thing is baseless. At the criterium race in the little Dutch town of Boxmeer, traditionally a chance for the media to get up close and personal with the year's Tour de France riders, a hungry press pack has its sights set on me. They ask about my blood profile, about the rift between me and the team. I deny everything and refer to the statement signed by Zorzoli. "There's nothing out of the ordinary. I have every right to compete. The UCI hasn't put the slightest obstacle in my way." As soon as I'm alone, the expletives erupt from deep within. I'm convinced the whole world is against me, furious with the UCI and furious with Rabobank; I take out my frustrations on my family and my girlfriend. I'm burning up inside yet still convinced my rage can spur me on to new heights on the bike. The only question now is for which team.

A few days after Boxmeer, I run into Bernhard Kohl at another criterium, the Draai van de Kaai in Roosendaal. We were teammates with the Rabobank Under-23s before going our separate ways. Kohl finished third in that year's Tour. Bernhard Kohl on the podium of the Tour de France—give me a break. The guy's a good rider, no question, but we both know he could never have hit those heights without pharmaceutical help.

As we ride over a quiet stretch of the course before the race, I mention that those Austrians apparently make incredibly good sports agents. It raises a chuckle. Then he tells me he had one more blood bag ready for the final days of the Tour but eventually decided not to use it because that really would've been too ridiculous. We have a good laugh about it, and for the first time in a long while there's a brief moment when I don't feel alone. That evening I go in search of more company. I pay Michael Boogerd a visit, just across the border in Belgium. I miss having him on the team and long for the good old days when we could break every rule without being held accountable by anyone.

We drink way too much that evening—Michael, his wife, Nerena, and me. Michael drinks himself senseless, and deep in the night, when the beer and the wine are slurring every word, he suddenly flips and starts accusing me of every mad act. In a fit of paranoia, he runs into the garden and crouches behind the bushes. When he tries to climb his garden fence, he crashes to the ground and lies there groaning, so wasted that Nerena fears the worst and calls an ambulance. Before long it pulls up at the house, sirens wailing, but Michael refuses to go with the paramedics. In the end he stumbles upstairs to bed and passes out.

The next morning I wake up with the hangover from hell. My tongue feels like a slug in a sandpit. I have an appointment to see Harold Knebel at Rabobank's swanky Amsterdam offices. The aim of the meeting is clear before we start: My contract is to be dissolved. Rabobank wants to get rid of me.

Knebel has brought a lawyer along. So have I. Jacques Hanegraaf is there too. The mood in the conference room is icy. I don't talk, I snarl. I'm a 23-year-old thug used to getting his own way, and Knebel is a middle-aged man used to giving orders. I understand now why the team wanted me out: I was a ticking time bomb. But at the time I feel like they're screwing me over. I see Knebel as a backstabbing banker who has no idea what he's talking about. I can't believe that they are willing to kick me out after the performances I put in that spring.

Fifteen minutes into the discussion, I say, "If I can't find myself another team I'll stay on. My contract covers next year as well." Knebel looks stunned and shakes his head. "No, not a chance. That's not on the table. You have to go."

They're so eager to wash their hands of me that they're willing to buy me out. The offer is my salary of €800,000 for 2008 paid as a lump sum and another €300,000 for 2009. Over $1.4 million just to fuck off. I take it.

My days at Rabobank are over. I arrived as a bright new talent; I'm leaving as a pariah.

21
DOING WITHOUT

IT SNEAKS UP ON ME. Silently, out of the darkness. A feeling I haven't had in years. I try to ignore it, but it's not going anywhere. Doubt. Season after season, my life as a cyclist seemed like a natural progression. I won more races, bigger races, my speed increased, my salary soared—but now everything's different. I am no longer Rabobank's rising star. I am a tainted rider in search of a team.

My mind is in two worlds at once. There are moments when I resolve never to dope again. But then I think about the blood bags waiting for me in Stefan Matschiner's freezer. Part of me wants to come clean about what I've been doing all these years, but I keep my lips sealed. Relations with Jacques Hanegraaf are at a low ebb; he's off running his own cycling team, Unibet, and I am no longer a priority. More than anything, I want to leave the past behind me. I tell Eelco and Martijn Berkhout to put out feelers and find me a new team, but I stop short of severing ties with Hanegraaf. Part of me wants to ditch him, knowing it was our alliance that set me on this road in the first place, but the rest clings to the old cycling ways of shots and pills, wheeling and dealing. And if anyone knows how to wheel and deal, it's Jacques.

I parted company with Rabobank on the assumption that other teams would be lining up to sign me, falling over each other to welcome me with open arms. The opposite is true. I'm a radioactive relic in a world where the major teams are out to avoid contamination at all costs. Eelco and Martijn reckon my best option is Slipstream, a US team making a name for itself in cycling's second division. They bill themselves as "The Clean Team" because many of their riders take an active stand against doping. It would be the best way to polish up my tarnished image.

The team is run by Jonathan Vaughters—an outspoken maverick who used to be a rider himself. Not just any old rider but a teammate of Lance Armstrong's and a fellow doper. He confessed his sins and has since set about giving riders the opportunity to ride clean. Eelco and Martijn know him and have tested the waters to see whether he might be interested in me. He is. It turns out that he has been following my career for quite some time and is even familiar with my junior and semipro results.

Vaughters has big plans for his team and sees me as the rider who can take Slipstream to the next level. He has only heard tell of my fluctuating blood values in passing. For an outsider it's virtually impossible to judge what's true and what isn't, not least because

Rabobank has issued a press release to the effect that there's nothing wrong with my blood profile. Meanwhile, I have supplied Eelco and Martijn with a copy of the statement signed by Zorzoli on the UCI's behalf. The Berkhout brothers are still finding their feet in the world of pro cycling, and I say nothing to enlighten them on the doping front. They only have a vague idea what all this talk of blood values means; the biological passport hasn't been in force for long, and only a select few grasp its implications. When they ask, I refer them to the UCI's signed statement: Not a cloud in the sky—Thomas Dekker has every right to compete.

At the end of July 2008, we meet Vaughters in Brussels. Our conversation is promising to say the least. He offers wads of money to win me over: a two-year contract with a salary rising from €700,000 to €1 million, excluding bonuses. He sets a number of conditions. I have to move to Girona in Spain and live in a villa rented for me by the team; many of the other Slipstream riders live in the region. I have to rent my Lucca apartment to Vaughters so he can be sure that I'm no longer living there. This is because he wants me to break all ties with Luigi Cecchini. "His image is doing you no good, Thomas," he growls. I agree to it all, and Vaughters is satisfied. He asks me to send him my blood values so he can go over them with the team doctor. We agree that he will hold a press conference in two days' time to announce the transfer.

We never get that far. One day after our meeting in Brussels, Vaughters calls Martijn. He has checked out my blood profile, and he's in deep shock. "You need to sit down," he tells Martijn.

"Those values—it's a fucking problem, man. The deal is off." He concedes that he can't prove that I've been doping, but he knows the odds are extremely high, and he wants nothing to do with that kind of rider. Martijn calls me up in confusion. He doesn't understand what has just happened, so I jump in my car and race halfway across the country to Haarlem, where Martijn and Eelco are based. As soon as I'm through the door, I admit the truth about the fluctuations in my blood profile. But I leave out the how and the why and dismiss Vaughters's fixation on blood values as bullshit. I play on their naïveté to make sure they continue their search for a team that will have me.

The brothers come up with two other options, both of them Dutch: Skil-Shimano and Vacansoleil. Both are competing one rung below the ProTour, a step down from Rabobank. At Skil-Shimano, a guy named Iwan Spekenbrink has just taken the reins. He expresses an interest, but he's not exactly beating a path to my door. Especially not when I refuse to supply the team doctor with my blood values. And when the Shimano riders say they don't want me on the team, it's the final straw.

That leaves one team and one team only: Vacansoleil. The team's boss is Daan Luijkx, one of the partners in an accounting firm that goes by the name of HH&L: Hanegraaf, Hoendervangers, and Luijkx. Hanegraaf is none other than my very own manager Jacques, who is married to Daan Luijkx's sister. Which is not to say they always get along. The brothers-in-law are locked in a conflict about money, and not long after I have spoken to Luijkx, the firm changes its name to H&L: the "H" of "Hanegraaf" disappears. Luijkx is eager to give me a contract. He has only just bagged Vacansoleil as team sponsor, and he's eager to make the leap to the ProTour at the earliest opportunity.

On Thursday, September 25, Martijn and I go to see Luijkx and his partner Hoendervangers at their office in Roosendaal. Luijkx does most of the talking. His hair is as black as the coffee served by his secretary. He tells me we share a common goal: to reach the top, as quickly as possible. I'm flattered by his interest, but just as we are winding things up, the conversation takes an unexpected turn. "Do you have those blood values under control?" Luijkx asks. "Of course," I answer. "I have a letter from the UCI stating that there's nothing wrong." He looks me straight in the eye and says without missing a beat, "So there are no more skeletons in the closet after that episode in Spain?" I nearly fall off my chair. Spain? What the hell . . . ? How does he know about Fuentes? Has Jacques opened his big mouth? "Nah, Spain's no problem," I stammer, and catch Martijn frowning at me. He has no idea what we're talking about. Luijkx seems happy enough. "Okay," I remember him saying, "and if not we'll figure something out together." I get the feeling that he genuinely has my best interests at heart, but it gives me the creeps that he seems to know so much about me. Things he has no right to know.

Fate steps in, and I don't end up at Vacansoleil. Another offer appears out of the blue, from the Belgian team Silence-Lotto. Sporting director Marc Sergeant gets in touch with Jacques Hanegraaf, thinking he's still the man in charge of my affairs. That bugs me. As time goes on, I want to have as little to do with Jacques as possible; what he knows can destroy me, just as I can destroy him. All the same, I'm glad that through him I have the chance to ride for a team that's racing at the highest level. At Lotto I'll be riding alongside the likes of Philippe Gilbert and Bernhard Kohl, who is moving over from Gerolsteiner. But Bernhard and I are not teammates for long: In mid-October, Kohl tests positive for the EPO variant CERA. He is banned and never makes a return to the peloton.

I sign my Lotto contract in Varese, Italy, where the world championships are being held. It feels strange to be there without taking part. Not that there would have been any point; I've put in next to no training, and my last race was back in July. I meet Marc Sergeant. There's not a lot of time to chat; we shake hands and sign on the dotted line. He doesn't ask a single question about my blood values, and he's willing to pay €400,000 for two seasons, about $590,000. Not only that, but I am allowed to bring a rider with me. I already have the perfect candidate in mind: Michiel Elijzen, a friend of mine and one of the few riders with the balls to take me down a peg or two when I start acting up. I nurture the unspoken hope that he'll be able to keep me on the straight and narrow, to some extent at least.

A few weeks after signing my contract I have a longer talk with Sergeant at his home in Belgium. He strikes me as a kindly man, his warmth underlined by a charming Flemish accent. As the conversation draws to a close, he says, "We're a well-behaved team. We don't get up to any funny business." I take this as a warning. But in that case I don't understand why he was so eager to sign not only me but Bernhard Kohl as well.

I'd like to say this was the moment when I decided to swear off dope for good. But it wasn't. I never did say a final farewell to the stuff. That said, I know I never want to go back to the way things were during my years at Rabobank. I can't handle the stress, the constant fear that the phone will ring and it will be a call from Switzerland telling me I've been caught. I want to get out there and ride, enjoy my racing again. And I know I can do it without doping. I readjust my ambitions, just a little. I am 24 years old. I have all the time in the world to build a career. I need to take better care of myself. Okay, so I might never win the Tour de France, but a couple of stage wins or the odd classic victory wouldn't be too shabby. I tell myself that cycling has changed with the introduction of the biological passport. That there's no longer the same need to get tanked-up on dope.

My appetite for racing returns, especially after a holiday in the Bahamas with Linda, Stefano Cecchini, and his girlfriend, Valentina. We wind up in a club that's well out of our league, and I end up shelling out €25,000. We drink too much. I do a line of coke. It goes on like that. But then, a few days later, I realize to my horror that I've started to develop a bit of a belly. I haven't done any serious training in a long time, and I'm itching to get back on the bike. I want to feel like a cyclist again, and I make an effort to get my life back in order. From the Rabobank payoff I buy a massive house in the Belgian town of Lommel, just over the Dutch border. The plan is to live there with Linda.

I head off to Spain for a training camp with Lotto. Flemish is the lingua franca on the roads and at the dinner table—close enough to Dutch for me to understand but different enough to make me feel like a bit of an outsider. Three-quarters of the riders are Flemish, guys like Greg Van Avermaet, Johan Vansummeren, and Leif Hoste. In the training sessions it soon becomes clear that I have a lot of ground to make up. For the past six months, I've been a slacker; my fitness level is so low it's gone underground. But I stick with the program—for now at least—and slowly but surely my condition starts to improve. My teammates are a fairly dedicated bunch. There's no alcohol at dinner—a lesson learned the hard way, someone confides to me later. During the camps a small group of us sneak away for the odd night out, but it's a far cry from my Rabobank days. We drink in clubs where the women flaunt what they've got, but we keep our bodily fluids to ourselves.

In the first races I'm there to make up the numbers. I take a nasty tumble on a training run, and I just don't have the form to compete for the honors. In the spring classics, I do the grunt work for Philippe Gilbert.

I see no sign of doping among my teammates, and it's not a topic of conversation over dinner, but then Belgian riders tend to be much more reserved than their Dutch counterparts. I do receive cortisone injections from team doctor Jan Mathieu for a series of bogus medical conditions, but that doesn't even register as doping anymore—for me cortisone is almost as much of a staple as sports drink in my water bottle. Mathieu comes up with a new injury every time; first it's my left knee, then my shoulder, then a saddle sore. When he talks about doses, he talks in terms of lines on the syringe. Each line is a 10th of a milliliter. On the Thursday before the Amstel Gold Race he injects five lines, and on the Saturday another two and a half. He gives me the shots behind closed doors, yet he talks about giving injections to other riders. It soon becomes apparent to me that this is a routine matter within the team. I can't say I'm surprised; my Rabobank years before the Rasmussen Tour were no different.

Gradually my form begins to come. I take fourth place in the Tour of Belgium, thanks mainly to a solid time trial. Then I head to Switzerland for my first ever block of altitude training, as preparation for the Tour de Suisse and the Tour de France. The altitude works its magic; the thin air jolts my body into producing extra red blood cells, and the Swiss Tour is the first race in ages where I can stay with the pace on the climbs. In the final time trial, I finish third behind Fabian Cancellara and Tony Martin. It's a weight off my shoulders. I still have what it takes, without the blood bags and Dynepo. At last—at long last—I'm back in the game.

A week before the Tour de France, I'm scheduled to ride in the Dutch national championships in Limburg. The day before, I drive down to Liège in my Porsche to receive a cortisone injection from Jan Mathieu. From there I drive to Landgraaf, where I'm staying at a hotel with Michiel Elijzen, Dirk Bellemakers, and Lotto team manager Hendrik Redant. After dinner we realize we still haven't picked up our race numbers. I offer to do the honors, jump in my Porsche, and zip over to the race offices. On the way back I lose my patience. I'm longing to get to bed, but I hit one red light after another. As soon as a little space opens up, I put my foot down on the accelerator. I must be doing around 90 kph when I see flashing blue lights in my rearview mirror. Police. I pull the Porsche over to the side of the road and lower the window. A cop my own age asks me for my car registration papers and ID, but everything's in my bag back at the hotel. I ask him if I can drive over and pick them up. Not a chance. I call Michiel and Dirk but there's no answer—they must already be getting their beauty sleep. I explain that I'm riding in the national championships the next day, but that makes no impression at all. I can mouth off all I like, but I have no choice but to accompany the boys in blue to the station, and I'm not allowed to drive there. Fuming, I get out of the driver's seat and into the back of the police car. Watching the young cop slide behind the wheel of my Porsche, I can't help myself. "Enjoy it while you can," I yell. "It's the only time you'll ever get to drive a car like that."

After another 20 attempts, I finally get Michiel to pick up the phone. His voice thick with sleep, he agrees after a good bit of persuasion to come down to the police station. Until he gets there I'm confined to a cell, stripped of my belt and shoelaces. The guy next door is off his nut on something, hammering on the walls and the door, screaming in a language that doesn't exist. When Michiel arrives with my ID and driver's license, the powers that be let me go with a €60 fine. I pay in cash. The young policeman at the desk asks if I can arrange a couple of VIP tickets for the national champs. I glare at him and say, "What do you think?" Shaking my head in disbelief, I drive back to the hotel. It's after midnight by the time I hit the sack, telling myself I'm still on course to become Dutch champion. But Michiel, Dirk, and I unknowingly destroy our championship hopes as we tuck into our scrambled eggs at breakfast: All three of us are felled by food poisoning. After 150 kilometers, I'm hunched at the roadside throwing up. The next day I can see the funny side. Food poisoning or not, I'm back in shape and I know it.

On Wednesday, July 1, 2009, I'm knocking about my apartment in Lucca, whistling a merry tune. It's 12:20, and I'm packing my bags for the Tour de France. I am raring to go, feeling no pressure, not a cloud on the horizon. No worries about prepaid mobiles and blood bags. It's finally starting to feel like I've turned the corner. Like the past is the past.

Then my phone rings. One glance at the display is enough. It's a call from Switzerland.

22
POSITIVELY POSITIVE

"HELLO."

"Hello, am I speaking to Thomas Dekker?"

"Yes."

"Hello, Thomas. This is Anne Gripper of the UCI's anti-doping commission."

"..."

"I'm calling to let you know that you have tested positive."

"What? Positive? What for?"

"Dynepo."

"Dynepo? But that's impossible."

"We have carried out what is known as a retrospective test and found Dynepo in a urine sample from 18 months ago."

"What? When?"

"Twenty-fourth of December 2007."

"..."

"You have until four o'clock this afternoon to inform your team, your family, and your friends. After that there will be a public announcement."

"Thanks for ruining my life."

"..."

Beep-beep-beep.

23

GIVE THEM NOTHING

I'M SITTING ON THE COUCH STARING INTO SPACE. No outburst. No tears. No anger or sorrow. I feel nothing. I'm a statue of a 24-year-old cyclist who doesn't know if he's still a cyclist.

I spend around 15 minutes in limbo. Then I pick up my phone and start pressing buttons like an automaton. Survival mode kicks in; I do what I have to do.

I call Kees and tell him I've been busted. I ask him to call my parents; I can't bring myself to talk to them, to hear the disappointment in their voices. Then I call Marc Sergeant to tell him he'll need to find a replacement for the Tour. I expect him to hit the roof, but he doesn't. He heaves a sigh, wishes me all the best, and that's that. I call Stefano and Luigi Cecchini. Stefano comes straight over—he lives just round the corner—and one hour later we're driving to Milan to meet a lawyer by the name of Cecconi.

While the six o'clock news in Holland is opening with the story of my positive doping test, I'm talking strategy with Cecconi. We agree that I'm not going to deny the allegations, but that I'm not going to tell all to the press. I will admit to blood doping and keep my mouth shut about the rest. Our aim is to keep the duration of the impending ban to a minimum; perhaps the authorities will be prepared to deduct six months for the time I wasn't racing while under contract with Rabobank.

Five days after Anne Gripper's call, I receive a registered letter. The sender is Jacques Hanegraaf. I tear open the envelope to find an invoice for services rendered: €58,000. No further comment. The message is clear. He's cashing in. He helped me arrange my doping, and now that I've been caught, he's dropping me like a hot brick. No phone call, not even a text message—he wants money and he wants it now. All before a single official sanction has been announced. I pay the invoice then and there. I want nothing more to do with Hanegraaf.

I spend a couple of weeks in an emotional no-man's-land, trying not to think about the past or the future. I eat like a robot, talk like a robot, take pills to get me to sleep. When I speak to Linda on the phone, I pretend that everything's under control. I don't want to make her more worried than she already is. I don't touch my bike, can't even bring myself to look at it.

I am summoned to a hearing in Monaco, where I am expected to give a full account of my actions to representatives of the Monegasque cycling association, who are in fact employees of the

French cycling association. They ask me if I acted alone. I lie and tell them I had no help from anyone. They ask me if I have seen other riders doping. I lie and tell them that I have seen nothing. I give them no details, no names; I give them nothing at all. The one thing they get from me is an admission that I have used blood doping—a term that covers EPO, Dynepo, and transfusions. I think it's smart to keep my mouth shut. I am the product of a system that expects you to clam up when the outside world asks about dope. I keep quiet because I want to return to the peloton one day; I keep quiet because I don't want to be the one to scare off Rabobank as a cycling sponsor and put dozens of people out of a job.

Above all, I don't want to be like Bernhard Kohl, sobbing into a microphone as he tells his sorry tale. I want to be stronger, tougher—far stronger and tougher than I really am. I want to be my own man. A macho man in a macho world. A man no one can touch. I maintain a stubborn silence and convince myself that it's the right thing to do. I'll sit out my ban and come back stronger than ever.

I'm not sure I believe it myself.

24

FALLING

FALLING IS DIFFERENT EVERY TIME. Sometimes you're facedown on the road before you know where you are. Sometimes it takes forever to hit the ground; from the moment you realize you're falling, one instant oozes into the next like molasses dripping from a spoon. You register the stones on the asphalt and the daisies among the grass, smell the massage oil on your legs, hear your spokes break in slow motion on the back of the rider sprawled in front of you. And before you hit the ground, you have the chance to wonder a thousand times whether you'll ever get up again.

After the phone call from Anne Gripper, weeks pass before I realize I'm falling. And once I realize, there's no stopping it. On and on I tumble, deeper and deeper. World without end, amen. I'm used to hitting the ground, feeling the pain, scrambling to my feet—but now there is no ground to hit. This pit is bottomless.

I run away. Linda comes down to Lucca for a few days, but as soon as she leaves, I hop on a flight to Ibiza, where Stefano has rented a house. I want to leave Lucca, get away from my bike, from Linda, from my parents. I want to escape from all the people I've hurt.

And I want to escape from myself. I start drinking. Not the occasional drunken binge like before, but every day. Too much every day. A few drinks early on smooth the jagged edges, and when I collapse into bed drunk in the small hours, my mind is no longer churning away, obsessing about the ban hanging over me. I go out every night. And I cheat on Linda with an endless parade of women. Tourists, waitresses, whores. Spanish, Italian, Russian. Women from God knows where whose names I don't even know. I'm a bruised ego in constant need of boosting. Every woman who falls for my pickup routine is like a race won. If only for a while, it helps me believe that I still count for something. I'm out to prove myself over and over again.

During my rare sober spells, all kinds of emotions rain down: anger, sorrow, frustration, regret, guilt. Mostly I hobble down the path of least resistance, clinging to the crutch of victimhood. Why me? What did I do to deserve this? After all, my sins were committed by countless others too. I wonder why my urine sample was tested retrospectively and not someone else's—as far as I know at the time, no other rider has ever been caught that way.

All summer I drift back and forth between Ibiza and Lucca, from beach to beach, from club to club. Out every night, spending money as though I have an infinite supply. It never even enters my

mind to put in some miles; my bicycle is home to a spider's web.
People ask me when I'm planning to start cycling again, and I tell
them tomorrow. But tomorrow never comes. Time stands still, and
I keep falling.

In late August 2009, Stefano and I head for the Tuscan coast.
I start drinking early. After a lazy day on the beach we hook up with
a motley bunch of pals and acquaintances at a nightclub called La
Capannina. You name it, I'm on it: wine, Cuba Libre, Champagne,
vodka. I piss away yet another small fortune, but I've stopped car-
ing long ago. I'm drinking to obliterate myself, to wipe myself out.
And when nothingness doesn't come fast enough, I pick up a can of
Red Bull and hurl it at a group of wealthy Russians sitting at a table
in front of us. A couple of them leap to their feet, pointing and firing Russian obscenities in my direction. I walk over to them. Out of
the corner of my eye I see the bouncer come running. I try to take
off my belt so I can lash out at him, but I'm too drunk to unbuckle
it. The bouncer gets me in a headlock, drags me toward the exit,
and chucks me out into the street. I lie there for a while, and then
my stomach starts to turn. I spew my guts up again and again.
I feel like it's never going to stop. Two hours I lie there gagging and
spluttering, until I'm completely empty inside. I don't know where
Stefano is, so a couple of guys I barely know drive me to a nearby
hotel in my Porsche and drop the keys off at reception. I wake up
the next morning wondering how the hell I got there and what the
hell happened. My temples are pounding, my skull hurts so much it
feels like some evil little gremlin drilling in my ear. As the hours go

by, my memory starts to flow, and gobs of the night before float to the surface. I can't face breakfast. I buy a bottle of iced tea from a machine and drink that, only to throw it all up again in the nearest toilet. I get into my car and look at my face in the mirror, a grayish shade of green. Sick as a dog, I drive back to Lucca, stumble into the apartment, and crash out on the bed.

I feel alone, so terrifyingly alone, that I book a ticket back to Holland. I want to go to Dirkshorn, to see Mom and Dad. I vow never to take another drink, to stop destroying myself. I touch down in Amsterdam the next day, and Dad is there to meet me at the airport. He hugs me, and I have to swallow hard not to burst into tears. Before he starts up the car, he rests his hand on the back of my neck, just like he did when I was a kid riding over to Grandma's.

At home in Dirkshorn, I start to recover, slowly but surely. But after a few days the restlessness kicks in and I head down to the Mysteryland dance festival. A couple of drinks later, I'm back in the saddle. I book a ticket back to Italy the next day, bid my folks fare-well, and—hey presto—I'm free to mess myself up all over again.

In October, my ban is announced: two full years with no reduc-tions. Twenty-four months without a single race. I can't bear to think about it. I've never been one for long-term planning; the day after tomorrow has always felt like a lifetime away. How am I sup-posed to get through two years? Two years or 2,000, it's all the same to me. The peloton is a long, long way off, nonexistent but for occasional contact with friends like Michiel Elijzen. I hear nothing at all from my former Rabobank teammates, and I'm too proud to give them a call. Only now does it sink in how little I've invested in other people as the years have gone by. I've allowed friendships to peter out, and now that I need friends more than ever, there's hardly anyone around.

I'm caught in the same vicious circle. I feel like a bastard for treating my girlfriend and my parents like shit, so I keep my distance. And to blot out the loneliness and the endless succession of wrong moves, I drink and end up acting like an even bigger bastard. Linda, my parents, Kees and Karien—they all offer me their support, but I shrug them off, taking out my frustrations on the people closest to me, reserving the worst treatment for the people I love the most. Love and hate become tangled in knots that can never be picked apart. It's more than just keeping my distance; I want to erase myself from their lives altogether. The days all look the same. I drink, go out, wake up around one in the afternoon, and start drinking again. I lose my license for eight months after being caught just outside Lucca's city walls in the early hours of the morning, driving home drunk from a nightclub.

I can't find the will to do anything. I have no purpose. There are no races to aim for, no ambitions to chase. I fall asleep with a feeling of gaping emptiness and wake up staring into the same void. At times I catch myself thinking I don't want to go on. That it wouldn't matter if I didn't wake up one morning. I never actually contemplated suicide, but if there had been a button to make it all go away, there's every chance I would have pressed it.

One year blurs into the next, and I go on a skiing vacation to Madonna di Campiglio. Seven months have passed since the ban, and I've been out on the bike a handful of times at most. It shows; I've put on 35 pounds. Sitting in a restaurant, I look down to see that the bulge above my waistline has popped three buttons on my shirt. The body I had the previous spring, when I was powering uphill with the best riders in the world, is nothing but a distant memory. Yet even the sight of my brand-new paunch isn't enough of a kick up the backside to get me out training again. Instead I signal to the waiter to bring another bottle of wine.

I've become a fugitive, constantly on the move. In the first year of my ban, I spend €150,000 on holidays alone. But no matter where I run, I take myself with me.

25
WIPED OUT

THERE'S NO HIDING IT. My blue cycling kit is straining at the seams. Last year it fitted me fine. Now I'm trussed up like a Sunday roast. I look at myself with a mixture of wonder and horror—my cycling mates Johan Vansummeren and Dirk Bellemakers are laughing so much they can barely stand. After 18 months of being a wastrel, this is one of my first serious attempts to get back on a bike. The three of us set off on a mountain bike trail somewhere in the woodlands of Brabant. I keep up for all of 500 meters; Dirk and Johan drop me before they've even hit their stride. There are two circuits, one 40 kilometers, the other 25 kilometers. They do 40, I do 25, and they still finish ahead of me. No wonder I feel like a loser.

The first winter of the ban, I don't train at all; any outings on the bike are short and sporadic. I ride when I feel like it, and that isn't often. Dirk and Johan live not far from my house in Lommel, and when they go out for a ride I try to tag along. Most of the time I'm barely hanging on. I can't keep up with them through the mud, and when they stick to the road it's all I can do to stay in touch.

I have no prospect of a new team. There are no offers, not even the faintest flicker of interest. I thought I would get a second chance if I kept my mouth shut, like the generations of busted dopers before me. But cycling has changed. The surge in doping scandals has put every team under a magnifying glass, and most of them are reluctant to hand out contracts to banned riders coming in from the cold. Those that do are often Spanish and Italian teams focused on resurrecting their own fallen heroes. I am neither Spanish nor Italian, and the team I rode for when I was doping wouldn't take me back if I paid them. It looks like my game plan has backfired big time; my silence is scaring teams off. Around me, other ex-dopers are starting to talk. David Millar speaks out, earns himself a second chance in the peloton, and goes on to write a book about his fall and his redemption.

Halfway through my ban and after a lot of hesitation, I give Martijn and Eelco Berkhout a call. It's been two years since I took advantage of my Jacques Hanegraaf connection and signed with Lotto behind their backs, and I know they think I screwed them over. Nevertheless, they agree to help me, albeit on their terms. One of those terms is that I talk. They want me to come clean, confess all. Tell the world what I've done and convince everybody that I'm not about to do it again. It means swallowing my pride, and I'm not sure that's something I want to do or am even capable of. It's a

difficult path, the road less traveled; I could always just stay silent
and hope some Italian B team will crawl out of the woodwork wav-
ing a contract. Then I won't have to say a word. I won't have to
look at myself in the mirror or admit I was wrong. The doubts keep
coming, wave upon wave, and just when I think I know what to do,
the tide comes rolling in again.

It's not a switch in mind-set from one day to the next; it's a
gradual process. Like one of those massive supertankers, I start
to change course little by little, and eventually Martijn and Eelco
talk me round. I open up, one chink at a time. A book is published
about me, and in it I reveal a few facts about my doping past.
I allow documentary maker Geertjan Lassche to film me for a
while, and I make a public statement about my blood doping—no
details, no names, no race numbers.

Sure enough, Martijn and Eelco come up trumps, and at the
end of 2010 they arrange an introductory meeting for me, with
none other than Jonathan Vaughters, whose Slipstream team has
found a new sponsor in Garmin. We meet at a Paris restaurant.
Once again Vaughters shows a genuine interest and we hit it off,
but after our previous encounter, he insists on full disclosure. He
keeps pressing me for more information. Stammering and falter-
ing, I come out with a list of banned substances. "EPO, blood bags,
testosterone, cortisone, Dynepo." He can't believe his ears. He's
been around cyclists long enough to know how things work, but
he didn't expect to hear that a young rider like me has been using
every banned substance going. I don't go into detail. I don't do that

with anyone. I'm caught between two worlds, sick of keeping quiet but still wary of spilling my guts. The truth I tell is the sketchiest version possible. Hypocritical maybe, but at the time it feels like a big step on very shaky ground. And eking out the truth in tiny doses is still better than lying.

In the winter before my ban comes to an end, I try to do something that resembles training. It's a hellish transition, and it takes me a long time to shed those extra kilos. My fitness improves at a snail's pace. I pedal away hour after hour but without a trace of conviction. It's more occupational therapy than serious training; without a team and a clear sense of purpose, I feel dead inside. I can't stop asking myself what it's all for, and the uncertainty eats away at me. I can't sleep, can't concentrate. I'm not living it for the full 100 percent—even 50 would be an overstatement. In hindsight, I should have gone back to basics, back to Holland, to Dirkshorn even, back to training behind my dad's scooter. But I don't. Instead I live life in fragments, shuttling between Lommel, Lucca, and Kees and Karien's in Luyksgestel without finding what I'm looking for anywhere. I fill my days with nothing. Sometimes I go on a bender out of sheer boredom or mope around the streets of Lucca feeling sorry for myself.

My plans to move in with Linda come to nothing. I put her off time after time. I tell her I need space to come to terms with my ban, but there's more going on beneath the surface. I jet around like a man of the world, but I'm still that little kid who's running from one family to another. How am I supposed to take care of

Linda when I can't even take care of myself? It's something I've never done. I've always been taken care of. No matter where I was, the world revolved around me. I can't even boil an egg. The ovens in my homes in Lucca and Lommel have never been used. I don't even own a coffee machine, and I can count my visits to a supermarket on the fingers of one hand. It's reached the stage where I only decide in the morning where I will be sleeping that same evening, depending on who has an empty bed and a full fridge. I've never washed my own clothes. The only domestic thing I do is at home in Lommel, vacuuming the carpet with a state-of-the-art Swedish machine. I vacuum in nice straight lines, for hours at a time. It's almost a compulsion, some semblance of order amid the chaos. But you can't suck the chaos out of your head with a vacuum cleaner.

In December 2010, I join Johan and Dirk at a training camp in Lanzarote. At least, that's the plan. The evening before we're due to fly out, I'm at Luyksgestel celebrating Karien's birthday and knocking back the white wine. They offer me a bed for the night, but I still have to pack and decide to drive home to Lommel. I still haven't got my license back, but that's a detail I choose to overlook. Lommel is only around 6 kilometers away; what could possibly go wrong? At around two in the morning I get behind the wheel of Karien's car—a MINI Cooper S convertible—and roar off into the wind and driving rain at 100 kph. It's a route I've taken a thousand times, and I know there's a hairpin bend coming up as soon as I cross the Belgian border. I take extra care when I hit it, but going into the next bend, my phone pings and the display lights up. I glance over at the passenger's seat for a second, and I don't feel my hands shifting a shade to the right at the same time.

Where the fuck did that tree come from?

The crash is explosive. The right side of the hood comes straight off, and the wheel is knocked out of my hands. The car rolls over again and again; everything around me spins. The air-bags shoot out, the windows shatter, and the rearview mirrors snap. In a flash I see a loose wheel flying through the air. I come to a standstill 150 meters farther on, the right way up. I look up at the black sky; friction has torn the roof clean off. The engine has died, and all I can hear is my own frantic breathing and the rain tapping on splintered glass. The airbags are red with blood. I feel a stabbing pain in my hand, and when I look down I see bone. Blood is pouring from the wound. I try to open the door, but I can't. I smash the rest of the window and squeeze out through the splinters. I'm so out of it that I get back in the car to look for my phone and try to restart the engine. It's only when I give up and I'm standing in the road a second time that I notice there is no car. The Mini is a heap of scrap metal with only one wheel still attached. I stare at the wreckage with my hands in my hair and wonder how the hell I survived this. Apart from that one deep gash in my hand, I appear to be all right. I walk around and see that the passenger's side has been smashed to pieces. I don't even want to think about what would have happened if someone had been sitting next to me.

I hear the sound of a car approaching. I wave and it stops. Two young guys stare at me wide-eyed. "Are you okay?" the driver says. I nod. "Yeah, but I need to get out of here. I've been drinking." The two exchange glances. "Us too." And off they race. I wrap my Gucci scarf around my bleeding hand and start to walk back to Luyksgestel. Slowly at first, legs trembling. But when I catch sight of the blue and red flashing lights of a police car in the distance behind me, I start to run. A doping ban is bad enough; the last thing I want is to wind up behind bars.

I run the 4 kilometers back to Luyksgestel, sick with fear. By the time I ring Kees and Karien's doorbell, I'm dripping with rain, blood, and sweat. Karien opens the door and gets the fright of her life. She begins to cry. Kees comes charging down the stairs in his underpants—he was already in bed. I am barely coherent. I start screaming that I've crashed the car and that we have to tow it away before the police find it. But it's much too late for that. Through the window we can see a police car turning into the street. "Lights out!" Kees yells, and barks at Karien and me to go upstairs and keep quiet. He pulls on some clothes, opens the door and steps outside. He walks up to the police car and says, "I've just had an accident. My son picked me up and drove me home. I'm still in shock. Have you seen the car?" The policeman shakes his head no. "We're from the Dutch police. Our Belgian colleagues asked us to pay you a visit." Thank Christ; if they'd seen the wreck they'd never have believed Kees could have squeezed his bulk through the window without so much as a scratch. The policeman gives Kees a Breathalyzer test; he doesn't drink a drop, so that's no problem. As soon as the police car has disappeared from view, Kees's son drives me to the hospital in Veldhoven to get stitches.

I miss my flight to Lanzarote; Kees drives Dirk and Johan to Charleroi Airport without me. I fly out to join them a few days later with my hand all bandaged up. My pals have nabbed the two best bedrooms in the hotel, and they consign me to a single bed in a tiny side room and tell me to reflect on the error of my ways. Oddly enough, I do as I'm told. The crash has shaken me out of my sleep-walking state. Getting behind the wheel of someone else's car with no license after an evening on the booze: How stupid can you get? It's all too clear what might have happened. How close I came to killing myself or someone else.

But it's more than just the shock; it's the shame. I'm stumbling from one near disaster to the next. My parents, Kees and Karien, Linda, the handful of friends I still have—all I seem to do is bring them trouble. I try their patience again and again. I understand Kees's kids when they tell him it's all well and good having that cyclist as a house guest, but there are limits.

I have no choice but to lie about the accident. I want to spare my parents even more worry, so I keep them in the dark. I tell Geertjan Lassche's documentary crew that I fell and put my hand through a window. But every time I twist the truth, I hate myself more. It's gone too far. Enough is enough.

Lie after lie after lie. I'm so fucking tired of it all.

26
LIFELINE

I THINK HE WAS THE COUSIN of the boy who lived across the street from us. He was chubby, wore thick glasses, and ran so slowly you had to look twice to make sure he was moving at all. When we played football on the empty lot around the corner, he was always last to be picked for a side. Maybe we took turns to be stuck with him—I can't remember—but the fat kid with the Coke-bottle specs never got near the ball.

Now, over 20 years later, I know how he must have felt. I am the four-eyed fat kid; no team wants to touch me with a bargepole. Not even when my ban comes to an end in mid-2011. There's still some vague talk of interest from Garmin, but apart from that the silence is deafening.

Out of sheer desperation I start riding local kermesse races in Belgium, just for the sake of something to do. Ralph Salden, one of the owners of a bike shop in Limburg where I stood with my nose pressed to the windowpane as a boy, supplies me with a bike, shoes, and kit: black and white, no sponsor. The first race I ride is in Sint-Niklaas. There's a church, a fast-food takeout, and 200 criterium riders lined up at the start. We ride what feels like a hundred thousand laps in a fog of massage oil and French fry fat—that's all I can remember. There is no satisfaction to be had. From the Tour de France to riding laps of Sint-Niklaas, it's another world. I feel like Lady Gaga reduced to playing karaoke night down at The Frog and Bucket.

In the weeks that follow, I line up for another 20 of these local free-for-alls. Kees and Karien chauffeur me around, Kees at the wheel and Karien in the passenger's seat with a bag of currant buns and cheese rolls. We crisscross our way through Flanders with Adele blaring on the radio.

August brings a ray of hope. Well, more of a glimmer really. The door to the pro peloton is inched open again by Jonathan Vaughters, but before he's even prepared to consider giving me a chance, he wants me to meet a whole raft of demands. He sends me an e-mail with a step-by-step plan. As soon as I open it, my heart sinks. He wants me to give a full and frank account of myself. In other words, I have to be as open as possible about my doping without triggering another suspension. He wants me to write to the World Anti-Doping Agency—WADA—offering my full cooperation and to persuade the president of the UCI, Pat McQuaid, of my good intentions. Vaughters wants me to talk to David Millar, a man he sees as a shining example of how to come clean and make a comeback after a doping ban. He wants me to undergo monthly blood tests and regular physicals so they can track my progress. I have to meet the CEO of Garmin, the team sponsor, to reassure him that he is not about to open the gates to a Trojan horse. I have to start at Chipotle, Garmin's development team, and I have to win the Duo Normand, a two-man time trial in Normandy, which Vaughters himself won in the dim and distant past.

I take the plunge. Not that I have much choice; I'm a drowning man and Vaughters's proposal is the only life preserver in the water. In early August 2011, I line up for the start of the Volta a Portugal as a rider for Chipotle. I make my return to official cycling in the prologue, where I finish 16th. I'm back in the racing game but I still feel like a fish out of water. I'm the oldest in the team, surrounded by guys who are five years my junior: Raymond Kreder, Alex Howes, Lachlan Morton—it's a new generation, and there's quite a gap to bridge. They are focused on cycling and nothing else.

For these guys, doping is a thing of the past, a long time ago in a galaxy far, far away. I envy them. Their innocence, their naïveté make me nostalgic for my 20-year-old self, the boy for whom everything in life seemed like a natural progression. Until he walked into that dimly lit hotel room with Fuentes.

But I am done with doping. I want nothing more to do with it. It has caused me so much trouble. My ambitions are scaled down. I no longer need to win a major tour. I'm happy just to be a cyclist again.

In the Volta, I'm left for dead. My body refuses to do what my brain wants it to do, and the Portuguese are riding with kerosene in their water bottles. A few days in, my knee starts playing up, a result of riding with pedals I'm not used to, and I pull out of the race. In the weeks that follow, I ride a couple of one-day events for Chipotle without any results to speak of.

None of this bodes well for the Duo Normand in the middle of September. For the time trial, I've been teamed with Johan Vansummeren. Kees drives us down to Normandy. The weather is foul, and the day before the race we train indoors on rollers while the wind howls outside. On race day, conditions aren't much better. We set off in the wind and rain under dark-gray skies, and we're soaked to the skin within minutes. Nevertheless, we pile on the pace. That is to say, Johan piles on the pace. He does three-quarters of the work up front while I die a thousand deaths hanging on to his wheel. But it's enough. We win.

Not the most spectacular of comebacks all told, but it's enough to keep Vaughters interested. I receive an invitation to join Garmin's pro team for their first training camp in Boulder, Colorado. Vaughters wants to see how I fit in. I fly to Denver in November 2011, and one of the soigneurs picks me up at the airport. We drive to the hotel, and when we arrive everyone is gathered at the dinner table. The worse for wear after the flight, I want nothing more than to collapse into bed, but I join them for a bite to eat. Some of the riders I know—Ryder Hesjedal, David Millar, and David Zabriskie—but others are new to me.

After dinner there's a team meeting, and I tag along to the conference room with the rest. Vaughters is already there. He says a few things about the sponsors and the year ahead, while I sit there nodding off in the back row. Out of nowhere, I hear my name. "And now I think Thomas would like to say a few words." Vaughters winks at me. "Come up here, Thomas." I jump and look around to see 30 pairs of eyes staring back at me. I get to my feet and walk hesitantly to the front of the room. You could hear a pin drop. I clear my throat and have no idea what I'm supposed to say. I've never felt so small or defenseless. "Hello, everyone," I stammer, hoping my English won't fail me. "I'm Thomas Dekker. I was banned for two years for doping. And uh . . . uh . . . I want to try and make a new future for myself in the world of cycling. And Garmin is a fine team." I mumble something else about a future in cycling and then grind to a halt. There's a lump in my throat. I stand there sweating and speechless in front of a roomful of cyclists and have no idea what else to say. Vaughters puts me out of my misery, and then David Millar and Christian Vande Velde come over and tell me they know how I must be feeling. I nod. I feel naked, stripped of all my pride. I don't know what Vaughters thought he was doing, but the truth is I would have done anything he asked. If he had told me to do 10 circuits of the room on all fours, I would have dropped to my knees and started crawling.

In the days that follow I'm part of the program. It's more about team building than training. The season has only just finished, and most of the riders are in their recovery period. We go mountain biking once, and on other days we go hiking in the mountains or compete to see who is fastest over an obstacle course. In the evenings we have a drink together. That's one talent that hasn't deserted me, so I'm right in there.

There's a strip club around the corner from the hotel, and we hang out there a couple of times. Some of the riders pay for a lap dance, and one evening I decide to join in the fun. I exchange a stack of dollars and take a seat. A blonde comes up and gives me a lap dance. Then she wants to give me another—I'm clearly a good tipper. But instead I say, "What's the point of that?" She looks into my eyes. "Yeah, you're right," she replies. "It would be much more fun to see each other after." She asks for my phone number.

A couple of hours later, I've already hit the sack when she texts me to ask if I'm still in the mood. I answer yes, and she texts me her address. There's a moment of doubt: I have to be down for breakfast at 7:00, and Garmin is my only chance for a comeback in the pro peloton. But my dick overrules my common sense. I pull on a pair of jeans and a shirt and slip away without waking my roommate. Outside I hail a cab and give the driver the address. He nods and we hit the road. Ten minutes, 20 minutes, half an hour. I ask him if we're nearly there, but he shakes his head and tells me it'll be another 30 minutes at least. The numbers on the meter continue to rise and one hour and $140 later we arrive in a little town called Lakewood. By this time it's 5:00 a.m. I get out of the cab and ring the doorbell of a small house. The blonde from the strip club opens the door in a T-shirt and jogging pants, and I follow her into the bedroom. The place is a mess, and it stinks of weed. I dive into bed with her and half an hour later all I can think about is my contract with Garmin. I glance at my watch and see that 5:30 has come and gone. I start to panic, jump out of bed, pull on my clothes, and yell at the blonde to call me a cab. After looking daggers at me, she complies.

It takes a lifetime for the taxi to arrive. I pace up and down the room and can't stop looking at my watch, picturing my contract sliding farther down the drain with every minute that passes. It's as if I'm trying my best to make that happen. This is more than just stupidity or refusing to see the consequences of my actions. It's a pattern repeating over and over: I'm sabotaging myself, destroying everything that's worthwhile in my life—my body, my career, my relationship, my friendships. And it feels like in recent years it's somehow been deliberate. I'm no psychopath—I have a conscience. I'm not an unfeeling macho or a bastard with no empathy. I'm not a bad person—at least I don't think I am—but my actions so often say different. Something inside is telling me I don't deserve the good things in life. A new contract, a loving relationship—I wonder if I'm worthy of these things. Part of me is out to sabotage my life as payback for the lies and the deception.

At long last, the taxi comes. I jump in, give the driver the address of the hotel, and ask him to step on the gas. We race through Colorado for an hour. The early morning glare makes the world look hard and raw. I'm a million miles from horny or drunk; all I can feel is a dull ache pulsing behind my eyes. At 6:55 we pull up at the hotel, and I ask the driver to drop me round the corner. I sprint through the front door and sneak through the lobby, hoping no one will see me. Passing the breakfast room, I can see the first riders already sitting at the table. I take the elevator to my room and find it empty; my roommate has already left. I know the only thing to do is pull on fresh clothes and run down to breakfast, but instead I sit on the edge of the bed with my head in my hands. Who am I trying to kid? At 7:10, someone hammers on the door. It's Charly Wegelius—one of the team managers at Garmin, who was also my teammate at Lotto for six months. Charly sees it's been a long night; the bags under my eyes are so heavy it hurts when I blink. I don't want to lie to him. "I've been an idiot, Charly." He shakes his head and shoves me under the cold shower. Five minutes later I'm at the breakfast table.

That same day, Vaughters comes to see me. He wants me to meet the owner of Garmin. I shake the man's hand and trot out a potted history of my cycling career. The man nods, Vaughters nods. I did good. My reward is a one-year contract with a salary of $45,000—elite cycling's equivalent of the minimum wage. I couldn't care less; for a chance like this I would have ridden for free. I sign my name and heave a sigh of relief. I am back to being a pro cyclist.

27

CARDS ON THE TABLE

I'VE JUMPED THROUGH NEARLY ALL OF VAUGHTERS'S HOOPS. The ones that remain all boil down to the same thing: I have to talk. He understands why I resorted to doping—he's been there himself, after all. What he can't accept is me keeping my mouth shut in my dealings with the French cycling association. It's a wrong he wants me to right, and so he packs me off to WADA with one very clear instruction: "Tell them."

No sooner said than done. On January 10, 2012, I find myself in a lawyer's office in Brussels sitting opposite a man in a sharp suit. His name is Olivier Niggli, and he is WADA's representative. Martijn and Eelco Berkhout are there too. I tell my story exactly as I told it to Vaughters. I list the substances I used but steer clear of the specifics.

As it turns out, Mr. Niggli is not all that interested in my past. He wants the lowdown on doping in the peloton right now. I tell him I have no idea; the last time I doped was a few years back. And for the past few seasons I have been nowhere near the peloton; I was off on a beach somewhere working on my paunch. He keeps asking, and I keep telling him I don't know. My true confession descends into a Monty Python sketch. After grilling me for an hour, he finally wraps it up. He says he'll be in touch and that WADA is eager to set up another few meetings with me. That's the last I hear of it.

The conversation with Niggli isn't exactly a breakthrough. But it helps put a little more distance between me and the omertà, cycling's age-old code of silence. I used to look on authorities like WADA as the enemy, and now I'm sitting across the table from them. What began as a goodwill gesture to Vaughters has become something more personal. I'm leaving behind my old self and the habits I picked up with my former teams. At Garmin they don't invent pretexts for therapeutic cortisone use; the team doctors aren't rooted in the darkest days of doping. Vaughters continues to champion the Clean Team ethos of openness and transparency. I'm not in a position to say whether it's a goal he has achieved, but he's certainly investing plenty of time and energy in making it happen. For me this is a completely new experience. We are encouraged to speak openly about doping. In my time at Rabobank, we were part of the system; at Garmin they are working to change the system. They can see that doping is choking the life out of the sport. That it's chasing away sponsors and fans. That it's chewing up talented young riders and spitting them out.

Vaughters is out to be the antidote to Lance Armstrong, to counter the old doping culture. Maybe he's being naïve, but his drive and enthusiasm are infectious. Vaughters has given me another perspective on doping. And that's just as well. Because I don't know what would have happened if I'd come back from my ban and been snapped up by a dangerous Spanish or Italian team. I'm pretty sure I wouldn't have gone chasing dope again, but what if the option had been handed to me? Can I say with my hand on my heart that I would have turned my back on forbidden fruits? I'm a chameleon. I adapt to my surroundings. If they're black, I'm black. If they're bright blue, you can count on me to be the biggest Smurf of them all. I tune in to what's going on around me, feed off signals, go in search of distraction. I'm the perfect guy to have at your table at a wedding; I can chat to anyone about anything and be genuinely interested. Politics, football transfers, art, cars, the financial markets, celebrity hairdos—give me my first question for 10 points and there's no stopping me.

My first race for Garmin is the Tour of Qatar. We win the team time trial, and I put in a decent performance, finishing 17th in the general classification. In the weeks that follow, I'm on a mission to ride as many races as I can to make up for my years out of competition. After Paris–Nice comes the Critérium International. I finish, but I'm not even a shadow of the 20-year-old who rode everyone into the ground. Next up is the Circuit de la Sarthe, a short stage race in France. On the final stage, I'm working hard to get our sprinter, Raymond Kreder, into a good position. I worm my way through the field, but when I notice that Kreder is no longer on my wheel, I launch my own attack. I glance over my shoulder and see daylight between me and the rest. To my amazement, no one catches me, and I clinch the stage win, just ahead of sprinter Nacer Bouhanni.

In the weeks that follow I notch up a run of solid placings in the Brabantse Pijl, the Amstel Gold Race, and the Bayern Rundfahrt. I'm starting to look like a contender again, and it fuels the hope that I really am on the comeback trail.

It's a vain hope. My progress stagnates, and before long I'm banging my head against a glass ceiling. As long as the races aren't too tough, I'm still a decent rider, but every hard mountain climb becomes a battle with myself. Part of the problem is physical. I'm weighing in at 165 pounds, when I should be 10 pounds lighter. But the key is psychological. I've lost that sense of invincibility. It's fear, not confidence, I feel when I line up at the start of the race. I long to be the Thomas I was before the dope, but that boy is dead and gone. There's only this Thomas, lugging his dark past up the mountain with him.

And there's another problem: I no longer live for cycling the way I should. The fanatical athlete in me is gone; the old spark has fizzled. If my training schedule says five hours, I put in exactly five hours. In the old days I would have done six. I let myself be distracted, time and again. I have different homes, different women.

Far fewer than I used to have, but it's still too much. In my doping days it didn't matter; a quick fix with EPO or a blood bag, and I was back on top of the world. But with the introduction of the biological passport, cycling has changed. You really have to dedicate your life to the sport if you want to excel. If your heart's not in it, you pay the price. I've entered a world where hardly any riders go on a bender at a nightclub or a brothel midseason. At training camps and before and after races, most of my teammates spend their time lying around in bed. Cycling has become more calculating and a damn sight duller. The sacrifices are greater than they used to be. I can muster that level of discipline if the rewards are big enough, but for me that means more than a stage win in the Circuit de la Sarthe or 18th place in the Amstel Gold Race.

If there's one thing athletes excel at, it's kidding themselves. I kid myself that I still want this, that I still have it in me—but all the while I'm making do with a supporting role. I continue to swagger around in the shining armor of self-assurance, but scratch the surface and it comes off like tinfoil.

I battle my way through the Vuelta a España; in the grupetto our uphill pace is so slow at times it's laughable. This isn't me, this isn't cycling. The only thing I gain in Spain is a new contract: Vaughters still has faith in me. I sign for two extra seasons with Garmin—for $100,000 in 2013 and $170,000 in 2014. It's nowhere near the kind of money I was once making, but it's a big step up from the ProTour minimum salary I've been on. To be honest, I'm happy with it.

There is one downside to my Garmin contract: Jacques Hanegraaf resurfaces, thinking there's money to be made, and slaps me
with a bill for over €90,000 in lost revenue. As he sees it, he still
has a right to a commission on the 18 months' salary I missed out
on when Lotto fired me for doping. It's a joke and a half coming
from the man who set me off down the road to doping in the first
place. I refuse to pay a single cent. We end up in court, and I win.

Shortly after the 2012 Vuelta a España, the world of cycling goes
into meltdown. The US Anti-Doping Agency—USADA, it's called—
issues a report containing hundreds of pages of testimony and
proof of doping within Lance Armstrong's U.S. Postal team. Tyler
Hamilton's revelations become the heart of a book that burns Armstrong's house of cards right down to the ground. Lance was king
of the mountain, and his fall drags other riders and teams down
with him.

Several of my Garmin teammates make public confessions,
among them Dave Zabriskie, Christian Vande Velde, and Tom
Danielson. The snowball gathers momentum, turning into an
avalanche that reaches as far as Holland when the USADA report
also mentions a number of Rabobank riders. For the bank, this is
the final straw, and it pulls the plug on cycling sponsorship. My
situation alters too. On the one hand, it lands me in the shit; the
past I thought I had left behind is raked up all over again, and I
find myself back in the spotlight as the doper who got caught. But
there's another side too. The revelations open a lot of people's
eyes. They finally start to see that I was no exception at Rabobank,

that there's only one real difference between me and many of the other riders: I got busted, and they didn't.

With Rabobank out of the cycling game, I no longer feel I have to keep my mouth shut to protect other people. Before, I was afraid that speaking my mind might rob the support staff, the mechanics, and the clean riders of their livelihood. But now there is no sponsor to appease. For the first time I see open road ahead and an opportunity to cast off the baggage I've been dragging around for years. The truth has been festering away inside me. I want to be free of it. I want to talk. Not just toss the press a bone or two to keep them happy, but throw off the whole rotting carcass. The pretexts, the lies, the hypocrisy—it all has to come out. And it's not just about me. I'm sick of a world where cycling—the sport I love—is always being haunted by its past. Unless the truth comes out once and for all, the stink from all the crap beneath the surface will never go away, and nothing will ever change. I hate to think of my nephew, just starting out in the cycling world, finding himself in the same situation I faced at 21.

In January 2013, I give an interview to Dutch daily *NRC Handelsblad* about my time at Rabobank, about the dope, my teammates, the team doctors. I admit that I was one of Fuentes's clients, that my alias was Clasicomano Luigi. I issue a press release stating that I will cooperate with an inquiry by the Dutch Doping Authority. On the day of the press release, I'm in the Spanish resort of Calpe, training to get myself into shape for the new season, when I receive a phone call. It's Michael Boogerd. I let it ring. I haven't spoken to him in a long time, and I have no burning desire to start now. He calls again. And again. In no time I have a dozen missed calls. He won't stop calling. But I've had enough. I've been caught and I've been banned.

I've kept my mouth shut for years, and this is where it ends. I'm no longer the guy who plays dumb to make other people's lives easier. I'm not going to keep lying so others will never have to face the truth. I want to live here and now, not in the past.

Eventually I send Michael a text message: "Enough is enough."

My interview with the Doping Authority takes place on February 4, 2013. The conversation gets off to a strange start. I'm there to help, but before I say a word, Herman Ram, the head of the Doping Authority, makes it clear that I will face further penalties if any new facts come to light. A further penalty could easily mean another two-year ban. It feels like a slap in the face. I've already been punished for my past, and I've steered well clear of doping since my ban. There is no incentive for me to put all my cards on the table; if anything, it's the opposite. Ram's threat casts a shadow over the entire exchange. Nevertheless, I tell him about everything I have experienced. I tell him about Hanegraaf, about Fuentes, about Matschiner, about Leinders and Van Mantgem, about the therapeutic-use exemptions for cortisone approved by Jan Mathieu. I tell him about Boogerd, not about his own pills and injections but about what he taught me, how he helped me obtain Dynepo and gave me Matschiner's number. I leave out one thing, the fact that I used testosterone, because those patches constitute a new fact and could lead to another penalty. I'm not about to be any-one's scapegoat. If Ram is out to punish riders or get his face on TV, then it's up to him to do his job.

When the new cycling season begins, I feel exhausted but lib-erated at the same time. I've thrown the weight off my shoulders; the ugly truth is out in the open at last. But it also feels like a farewell. A farewell to the past but maybe the start of a farewell to cycling itself.

28
ASHES AND EMBERS

I AM ALONE. All I can hear is my breathing and the whizzing wheels of my time trial bike. It's early afternoon—way before the TV broadcast is due to begin, way before the star riders launch their bid for glory. Spectators are few at this time of day. The handful of people at the side of the road gaze glassy-eyed as I ride past. No one shouts my name. Once upon a time I looked forward to days like this; I lived for time trials. But once upon a time has long since gone. In the 2013 Giro d'Italia I'm nothing more than filler for the peloton, even in the time trial. It's been a long time since I've given my all. I pedal to the finish in Saltara because I have to. I finish 135th, almost eight minutes behind Alex Dowsett and Bradley Wiggins.

In my first years as a cyclist, I had a sacred flame burning inside, a flame that erupted into a raging fire. But in 2013 the fire is all but gone. A sacred flame is a flame like any other: Without fuel, without oxygen, it flickers and dies. You have to stoke the fire. And that's something I have failed to do. There's nothing left inside but ashes and embers.

I train on automatic pilot, race without any ambition. Martijn and Eelco have hooked me up with a coach in an attempt to give my career a new boost. He's Greek—Vasilis Anastopoulos is his name, but everyone calls him Vasi. He sets about structuring my training and sharpening my focus, but I don't do half of what he tells me. I drag myself from race to race. Cycling may seem like a sport where it's all about who has the strongest legs and the biggest lung capacity, but the psychological factor is far more important than most people imagine. You have to want to drive yourself hard and push beyond your pain threshold. You have to be able to ride yourself into the ground. I can't do it anymore. I've lost faith. Self-doubt is firmly lodged in my brain. When I hit my limit on a mountain climb, I think I'm the only one. Before my doping ban I would have attacked, secure in the knowledge that everyone else was hanging on by their fingernails as well. It's as if I have become another person. There was a time when I never had to think anything through; it all came naturally. Now I find myself lying awake obsessing about the smallest details.

Within the team, it's clear that riders like Dan Martin and Ryder Hesjedal are way better than me. They ride fast in the races I used to ride fast in. My own racing amounts to little more than lending a helping hand. I work for the team, get dropped in the final stages, and make my way to the finish. It's a part I resign myself to playing because I have no choice. No one on the team sees me as anything other than a domestique. There are training sessions when I'm about as much use as a wet newspaper, but no one takes me to task. During Liège–Bastogne–Liège I spend the whole day shielding Dan Martin from the wind. He goes on to take the win. I'm delighted for him and for the team, but deep down it doesn't give me any fulfillment. I'm not used to riding for others all season.

Yet it never occurs to me to quit. Cycling is my security blanket. It's all I know, it's what I do. I've never done anything else. I have no qualifications, I've never learned a trade. Without cycling, I wouldn't have a clue what to do with myself. And so I keep on cycling.

Training, eating, sleeping, racing—I'm stuck in a rut, devoid of all conviction and enjoyment. Off the bike too, life is pretty boring by my standards. There are no more wild parties, and I seldom drink myself into a stupor. I go off the rails less than I used to. Not performing at my best means I have less of an urge to let myself go. If I go out at all, it's to relieve the boredom, not because there's anything to celebrate.

For one fleeting moment I feel as if I still have what it takes. At the end of 2013 I spend week after week on the road with the team for a series of training camps and races in North America. Without any distractions and the temptations back home, my fitness improves rapidly; I'm leaner than I have been all year. But on a ride to check out the prologue to the Tour of Alberta, I overlook a hole in the road and go flying over the bars. Pain immediately flares up in my left knee. Garmin's team doctor says there's no need for me to go to the hospital, and so I ride on for days with a swollen knee, first in Alberta and then in the Grand Prix Cycliste de Québec.

I'm in pain—a stabbing pain that won't ease up—but Vaughters forbids me to quit or go home. I do it anyway. In Québec I book myself a flight to Paris and from there catch the TGV to Brussels, where Kees picks me up. We drive straight to the hospital in Veldhoven, and they give me an MRI scan. My tibia is broken. I send Vaughters an e-mail with the details of the scan, but I don't even get a reply. Maybe it's an intentional snub, or maybe he's just busy, but I draw my own conclusions: I am not an important rider in his team.

29
ADRIFT

FIVE YEARS LATER THAN PLANNED, it happens: Linda and I move in together. She puts me on the spot. She's had it with all the delaying tactics, and she's willing to give us one more try, but only if it's for real. Either we call it quits or we move in together. It ends up being the latter.

For years our relationship has been on and off. At times I'm not even sure whether it's on or off. There's always something pushing us apart. I could tell you we're both at fault, but I'd be lying. Nine times out of 10 it's me. I cheat on her, I get caught for doping, I come home plastered, I nearly kill myself in a car crash—in sabotaging my own life, I sabotage our relationship as well. It's always under stress, there are always bizarre incidents or accidents. I can't get to grips with my own life, never mind my life with Linda. And she can't get to grips with me. Yet for all the problems, it's clear as day: We love each other heart and soul.

Linda is my oasis. Whether it's over dinner or on the phone, we can talk for hours on end. We call each other countless times a day; when she's driving to the Eindhoven law firm where she works, on her way home. In a very real sense, we are simply there for one another—she's more my rock than I am hers, but still, Linda is one of the few fixed points in my life. No one knows me better than she does. She is one of the few people who can hold up a mirror to me. She can put me in my place, and she knows how to get through to me. When she talks, I honestly listen. Only I don't always act on what she says.

In October 2013, Linda moves into my house in Lommel. It's a good move and a bad move at one and the same time. It feels good not to be alone, but however much I love her, I find living together complicated. I'm a far cry from the egotist I used to be, but I'm no saint either. Now that I'm sinking ever deeper into a rut with my cycling, I go in search of other things to excite me. And the things that excite me most tend to wear short skirts and high heels. I know it's stupid, and I know I'll regret it, but I do it anyway. One woman is not enough. I'm excessive and destructive to the core.

That winter I'm away for months on end. I travel from training camp to training camp, and my season starts in January 2014, on the other side of the world. I ride Australia's Tour Down Under followed by the Herald Sun Tour. In February I spend a couple of weeks at home before I head down to the Tirreno–Adriatico. The night before my flight to Italy, Linda happens to see a text message on my phone. It leaves little to the imagination; I've been up to my old tricks again. I try to talk Linda round. I apologize with everything I have in me, and I leave for the Tirreno with the hope that I can put her heart back together again. I try to concentrate on my racing, but a few days later she texts me late at night. She has packed her things and gone. And she is never coming back.

I lie awake until five that morning, staring at the ceiling. By the time I climb onto the bike a few hours later for a stage of 200 kilometers, I'm a wreck. My legs pump away like pistons, but my head is somewhere else. I am sad, dejected, and disappointed in myself. I've blown it. If anyone in this world knew me, it was Linda. If anyone could give me solid ground beneath my feet, she was the one. And now that she's left me and left for good, I can't even blame her.

There was only one problem with our relationship: the fact that I was in it.

30

THE STUPIDEST IDEA EVER

MY KNEE HURTS. My legs hurt. My heart is broken. It's August 2014, the Tour of Utah. My teammate Tom Danielson is leading the general classification. I've been cycling with my head in the wind for days. Tomorrow is the final stage, but I'm not going to wait until then. They can get through one last day without me. As we pass the hotel, I squeeze the brakes and make a U-turn. I've barely ridden a decent race all season. I'm not half the rider I once was. My body has already said farewell to cycling, and it's waiting for my head to catch up.

I'm a cyclist on paper only. My heart says different. A few months earlier I pulled out of the Giro d'Italia during a stage that was plagued by snow and hail. We had agreed among ourselves to call a truce in those conditions but ended up racing anyway; we plunged into descents while the snow frosted up our glasses. It was madness, and I suddenly saw the insanity of my chosen profession. What the hell were we doing? What the hell was I doing? I got off the bike. Same as now, here in Utah. I roll back to the hotel in Park City with an air of quiet resignation. I take a shower and lie down on the bed, only to wake up hours later. Since there's no more racing for me the next day, I decide to head into town.

I wind up at a place called the No Name Saloon. It seems like the right spot for me. Here I have no name. No one knows me, no one cares. I'm just a bit player in some race that's passing through. I pull up a bar stool and order a drink. Before I've drained my glass, never mind placed another order, a fresh drink appears in front of me, courtesy of a guy farther up the bar. He slips me a wink, and I wander over to thank him. He's with two other men and a woman— a beautiful woman. She introduces herself as Nathalie. For the rest of the evening I can't take my eyes off her. She's intelligent and charming, but there's something elusive about her. I couldn't begin to guess her age—and it doesn't matter to me either. I head back to the hotel around two, but not before I get her number. I text her the next day to ask if she wants to meet up, and that evening we go out on a date. We talk endlessly. She turns out to be almost 20 years my senior. She lives in Los Angeles, deals in art, and produces films. She has three daughters and used to be married to the founder of the clothing brand Guess. I melt when she looks at me. The worlds we come from are light-years apart, but I've seldom felt closer to someone I've just met. We end the evening at an altitude of 10,000 feet, in her holiday home at the foot of a ski run.

A few weeks later we meet up again, this time in Amsterdam. We visit the Rijksmuseum and the Anne Frank House, we go out for dinner, and stay at the Pulitzer Hotel. We have so much to say to each other. She knows nothing about cycling and had never heard of Thomas Dekker until we met—and that's just fine with me. She has a whole different view of the world. She has lived life to the full, and nothing seems to faze her. I can talk to her about anything and everything, and it dawns on me that I'm falling in love. In the weeks that follow I call her so often it's like my phone has been grafted to my ear.

All the while, my relationship with my bike grows colder. I pedal my way to the end of the season without giving it much thought. The team goes from strength to strength, but I'm just a small cog in the machine. I quit the Giro di Lombardia early and watch Dan Martin's win on TV in the team bus, long after I'm showered and done for the day. Late in October, I find myself in China for the Tour of Beijing. The final stage begins on Tiananmen Square and has us circling the Bird's Nest Stadium about a hundred thousand times. I finish 74th. Little do I know it's my last result as a professional cyclist.

For months Martijn and Eelco Berkhout have been trying to pin down Jonathan Vaughters on the subject of my contract, which is up for renewal. But Vaughters won't commit. Garmin merges with an Italian outfit called Cannondale, and Vaughters finds himself with too many riders to fill too few places. He keeps putting off his decision, and I'm left dangling. I know better but continue to hope it will all turn out for the best. I jet off to Miami on holiday and to see Nathalie. When I return, Martijn breaks the bad news. "Jonathan isn't going to renew." I'm disappointed in Vaughters for not taking the trouble to call me personally, but I understand why a new contract isn't in the cards.

There is no plan B. Over the preceding two years, my results have been all but nonexistent. It would take a miracle to find me a new team. Sleep won't come that night, and I lie there staring into the dark, feeling lost, worried for the future. What now? I don't want my life as a cyclist to end. More to the point, I don't want it to end like this. Not as the guy who finished 74th in the final stage of the Tour of Beijing. I don't want to just drift away over the horizon, carried on the wind like an empty plastic bag.

A few days later, Martijn calls me up. "Thomas, we have a plan. A way to prove you can still ride fast. To other teams and to yourself." I frown. "Well, what is it?" Martijn answers, "An attempt on the Hour Record."

It's the stupidest idea I've ever heard.

31
THE ATTEMPT

I COULD HAVE TAKEN THE EASY WAY OUT and told Martijn and Eelco they were out of their minds. I could have left their Hour Record idea for what it was and just announced my retirement one sunny day. I could have pretended none of it mattered to me anymore. Jetted off to an island in the sun and lain on a beach for months on end, drowning in cocktails and self-pity.

I could have but I didn't.

For the first time in years, I start swimming against the tide. I know it's going to take months of training and searing pain. I know there's every chance I'll fall flat on my face. But the longer I walk around with the idea of the Hour Record attempt in my head, the more it takes root. I look into the history of the event and discover that the record was once held by Miguel Indurain. It dawns on me that this is my chance to join a roll call of cycling greats. The UCI modified the rules a while back, and now riders are permitted to chase the record on a time trial bike. The current holder is Austria's Matthias Brändle, who records a distance of 51.852 kilometers in 60 minutes. Brändle is a good rider who has easily outclassed me for years, but he's no Superman. I know that Bradley Wiggins also has his sights set on the Hour Record and that there's every chance he'll blow Brändle clean out of the water. If I have any hope of claiming it for myself, even for a short while, I have to make sure I beat Wiggins to the punch.

In November we hold a meeting in Eindhoven with a group of specialists put together by Martijn and Eelco. The team consists of a coach, Vasi; two human movement scientists, Leon Burger and Jim van den Berg; and a track cycling expert, former points race world champion Peter Schep. Peter doesn't pull his punches. He hasn't seen me deliver a decent turn of speed for years, and he wonders if I've still got what it takes. The rest think I can do it—in theory—but everything has to be just right. Above all else, I have to reinvent myself compared with recent seasons. Three and a half months is all I have to prepare. I need to train like mad and dedicate my life to cycling again. If I can't put in the hard work, then we're on a road to nowhere from the start. I take a solemn vow to give it my best shot. I have no way of knowing if they honestly believe me. I hope they believe me. I hope I believe me too.

On a cold afternoon in the depths of winter I do a lab test with Jim and Leon to see what kind of shape I'm in. It's a nightmare, bad news from beginning to end. My body fat is over 15 percent, and my power output is 355 watts at threshold. If I want to have a chance at the record, I'm going to have to up that by around 60 watts—and then sustain it for a solid hour. Jim scratches the back of his head and says, "Well, let's just say there's room for improvement."

Training gets off to a shaky start. My confidence has taken a knock, and the day of the record attempt still seems such a long way off. In no time the schedule starts to feel like a straitjacket, and I begin to needle Jim and Leon about the sessions: They're too much, too tough, too early in the day. But on every task they set me, I deliver. I fly to Greece for a training camp. I do endurance work on the road, intensive sessions on the track, and customized power training three times a week with Tom Boonen and Johan Vansummeren. I swear off the booze completely. There's almost always someone with me when I train. Vasi, Jim, Leon, and Peter watch me like a hawk. I can't worm my way out of anything; there's nowhere to hide. If I don't push myself hard enough, I can always count on getting a kick up the backside. And when I do my best, there's a pat on the head. It's not rocket science but it works. I get better. And better. And better. My test scores improve, and I start to get used to my Koga bike and the aerodynamic position I have to maintain. Even so, it still feels like I'm riding with my tongue on the front tire.

Two months in, I begin to feel something I haven't felt in a long time. Something that feels a lot like self-belief. My confidence builds, and this time I'm not bluffing. I start talking myself into winning mode and tell everyone who'll listen that I'm going to break that record, that I can take Brändle easy. For years I've been making do with a dying ember; now the flame is burning bright once more. At last I'm back to being a cyclist.

There is a shadow side to this new lease on life. While it feels grand to be powering away on the bike again, confronting the truth isn't easy. The numbers show a 17 percent improvement in less than three months, the kind of progress you'd expect from a Sunday cyclist, not from a pro. The cold, hard facts are staring me in the face. Living for cycling again triggers memories of how I trained before I turned pro and the superhuman effort I put in during my first years at Rabobank. How many years have I frittered away since? Letting it all slide, sitting back, and watching my career crumble.

I'm glued to the TV screen as two Australians set off on their bikes in a bid to break Brändle's Hour Record. Jack Bobridge doesn't make it and caves with 15 minutes to go. But Rohan Dennis is another story. He breaks the record and raises the bar to 52.491 kilometers. It's nothing short of a body blow for me; it means I'll have to go even faster than planned. At that moment, Dennis is one of the best in the world. He's blown me away in almost every time trial over the past few seasons. And I can't help noticing how much both Bobridge and Dennis suffer along the way. It confirms all my fears. Those 60 minutes of lap after lap are going to be pure torture.

My fears are compounded when I do a test run at the velodrome in Alkmaar, scene of my boyhood training sessions. I step into the arena with a sense of nostalgia. Breathing in, I can smell the past.

With my parents and a bunch of friends up in the stands, I complete the test at 90 percent capacity. It goes well, but when I get off the bike at the end, my hamstrings are tough as old boots and my backside is a solid lump of compacted muscle. It's like I've spent the past hour bouncing around on a pneumatic drill.

I stagger into the showers, and when it comes time to dry myself off, I can't reach below my knees. I struggle into my clothes and have to leave my shoelaces unfastened. The biggest humiliation is yet to come. I love my Porsche, but now that low-slung suspension is mocking me. My wrecked hamstrings and compacted ass refuse to cooperate. I can't get into my own bloody car. Eventually I have to get down on my hands and knees and haul myself in—and even that's a challenge. I'm in so much pain that there are tears in my eyes as I pull onto the highway heading home to Lommel.

I'm only just under way when the fuel tank indicator lights up. I swear and stop at the next gas station on the A9. I heave myself out of the Porsche, fill her up, and hobble over to the cash desk and back. So far so good, but now I have to find a way to get back behind the wheel. By this time my hamstrings have seized up to the point where they might snap at any minute. It doesn't matter what shapes I throw, my ass isn't even close to connecting with the driver's seat. Not knowing what to do, I give my old pal Dirk a call; he and a friend were at the trial run in Alkmaar. They are already on the other side of Amsterdam, but he turns the car around, bless him. Once he arrives, he drives me home, while his buddy tags along behind at the wheel of the Porsche.

The day after the trial run, my fucked-up hamstrings and I join
Leon Burger on a flight to Mexico. We're off to take advantage of
my secret weapon: altitude. I am going to launch my attack on the
Hour Record at the cycling track in Aguascalientes, 2,000 meters
above sea level. The advantage is lower air resistance; the catch is
that there's less oxygen in the air. Acclimatization is essential, and
so we have set aside two weeks for that process. I train at a steady
pace, and we fine-tune the equipment. Nathalie pays us a visit. She
is struck by my determination but also by how nervous I am. My
record attempt will be broadcast live on TV and online. Everyone
can see what I make of it. This could be the comeback of a lifetime or a crushing humiliation. I don't even want to think about
whether it's my last hurrah as a cyclist.

The big day dawns: February 25, 2015. As soon as I open my
eyes, nervous energy starts coursing through my body. I'm like a
teenager before his first driving test. Five minutes after breakfast,
I'm staring into a toilet bowl. Every mouthful has come back to
haunt me. On my way to the track, I can feel how hard my heart is
thumping. It's sickening and magnificent at the same time. I never
thought I'd say it, but I've missed this jangle of nerves.

Vasi, Jim, Leon, Martijn, and Eelco are already waiting track-
side. They have come all the way to Mexico for my sake, and it
means the world to me. The stands are filled with local schoolkids.
I warm up on the rollers. Down in the catacombs, I squeeze into
my skinsuit and pull on my socks and shoes. As I put on my helmet
I whisper to myself, "Come on, Thomas." My bike is standing ready

on the boards. I climb on and wait for the moment. The first songs from the playlist that Nathalie has compiled for me are coming over the sound system loud and clear. The pistol sounds, and I haul myself into action.

My muscles are raring to go, my lungs unfurl. For the first 20 minutes I barely even feel my legs. I am riding to Rohan Dennis's schedule, knowing full well that the worst is yet to come. As the hour ticks away, the minutes begin to stretch. My heart rate climbs, my breathing becomes heavier and then heavier still. After 40 minutes, exhaustion strikes. I'm ready for it, I know it's coming, but it still feels like a crippling blow to the neck. Cycling becomes battling, pedaling becomes plodding. In a regular time trial there's always the chance to ease the pressure for a second or two—if only on a bend—but caught in this loop on the track, there's no letup. The pressure builds and builds. My tongue is hanging farther and farther out of my mouth. With every bend, I wobble more. My heart rate is climbing toward 200 bpm. Everything hurts. Back, legs, and most of all my lungs. I am gasping for breath like a stranded goldfish. I ask myself when I have suffered this much, and there's no answer. This is torture. I have to keep my lap times down, but I just can't do it. I begin to lose precious ground to Dennis. A little at first, then a little more. The final minutes are a battle for survival. I dig in and squeeze every last drop of effort from my body. If I'm going down, I'm going down with guns blazing. I taste blood. My lungs are about to explode, my legs are screaming for mercy.

And then it's over.

I fall short: 271 meters short to be exact; 889 fucking feet. I am spent. Completely wasted. Someone helps me off the bike, and I sink to the wooden track with my head in my hands. After a few minutes, I struggle to my feet and head for the changing room. I burst into tears. I am so tired, so indescribably tired. It's not just the record attempt, it's everything—all the pain and frustration of the past couple of years. I'm frustrated that I didn't make it, but there's a sense of pride at the same time. I've achieved something I haven't been capable of in years. I've lost to Rohan Dennis, but it's a victory over myself. I can't turn back the clock and make up for all those lost years of training. I can never be the Thomas Dekker I once was—but fucking hell, I still have it in me.

32

BIG TALK, SMALL TALK, NO TALK

I'M SLUMPED IN A CHAIR staring out at the plane that will take us from Mexico City back to Amsterdam. It's all I can do to keep my eyes open. The whole team went out for a night on the town in Aguascalientes, and it was a long one. About time too, after three and a half months of living like a monk, but I drank so much that my memories of that night have been sucked into a big black hole.

My phone rings, and I glance at the display. It's Michael Boogerd. I haven't spoken to Michael in a long time. He bitterly resented me dishing the dirt about everything that went on with Rabobank. But since he went public about his own doping past, the frost has thawed a little. I pick up.

"Hey, Michael." "Hey, Thomas." It's familiar and awkward at the same time. There's tension between us, but there's also a bond of sorts, based on all that we've shared in the past. He tells me I gave the Hour Record a damned good shot. He didn't think I had a performance like that left in me. After that it's all small talk until the conversation turns to Roompot—a new Dutch cycling team. Michael is one of the founders. He tells me he's pumped a shitload of his own money into the venture and that he can see to it that I get a place on the team. "Sounds good," I say. We agree to meet up in Holland before long.

In the months before my record attempt began, fear had been my only reason to remain a professional cyclist. I had no idea what else to do, petrified of a life without cycling. But after taking on the Hour Record, everything has changed. I actually want to be a cyclist again. I still don't know whether I can stick to the training schedule and the lifestyle, but the last few months have set me free. I'd love to ride for Roompot, even though they're not operating at the highest level or competing in all the big races. But the Tour de Luxembourg and the Ster Elektro Tour are worth winning too. At least, that's what I tell myself.

Martijn and Eelco have been in touch with Roompot's management team for a couple of months. Alongside Boogerd, it consists of Erik Breukink—yep, the ghost of Rabobank past—former sprint hero Jean-Paul van Poppel, and rider turned manager Michael Zijlaard. Initially they keep stalling, insisting they don't have the money to pay me. That's bullshit; the days when I played hard to get are long since gone. My motivation now is pure and simple: I still have unfinished business in the world of cycling. In the wake of my Hour Record attempt, it's Michael Zijlaard in particular who's tempted to take me on—if only for the publicity it could generate. He holds talks with my management, and a meeting of the minds looks to be not far off. They agree that I should have a word with Breukink and Boogerd in person. If they give the green light, there's nothing to hold us back.

In early March I pay Breukink and Boogerd a visit. I try to play it cool, but I still feel like a schoolboy called in to see the headmaster. I am prepared for a cross-examination, a barrage of prickly questions and recriminations. But I couldn't be more wrong. It's like talking to a couple of old pals at the bar. How's things? Fine, how's life been treating you? They ask me what I think of riding for a team where things aren't organized for you down to the last detail. I tell them I don't mind at all. I try to convince them that my love of the sport has been rekindled, that I'm no longer the rider of recent years who hung around at the back of the peloton, who had lost his appetite for racing. They listen, they nod, and they tell me they'll call me the next day once they've had a chance to talk things over with the full management team. I leave thinking I'm as good as signed. After all, Boogerd made a point of calling me after my record attempt to tell me he'd love to have me on the team, and I've never known Breukink to row against the tide. All things considered, what could possibly stand in my way?

The next day I get a phone call at around seven in the evening. Not from Boogerd, not from Breukink, but from Martijn. "They're not going to do it, Thomas." The first thing I do is call Boogerd. I'm pissed as hell, and I don't try to hide it. Michael asks if he can call me back. "I'm taking my son to football practice." Eight o'clock comes and goes. Nine o'clock. Nine thirty. By this time I'm climbing the walls. Come ten o'clock I can't take it anymore, and I reach for the phone. "Football practice over yet?" I ask, laying on the sarcasm. His only response is: "They don't want you on the team, Thomas." "So what was all that stuff about you being able to sort it out?" I ask. Faintly, he mumbles, "No, you don't get it. There's all sorts of shit coming down. The UCI is after me." All I can say is, "I guess we haven't heard the last of each other." I hang up.

I'm sick of it all. Sick to my stomach. The beating around the bush, the bullshit, the lies, and hypocrisy. I'm sick of Boogerd, who has never been penalized but acts like he's the victim of a witch hunt. I'm sick of depending on other people, sick of the past, the doubts, the uncertain future. I'm sick of having to beg for a contract, of trying to convince myself that I still want this life. I'm sick of pretending, of hoping against hope. I'm sick of putting off the decision, tormenting myself, comparing myself to the athlete I once was. I'm sick of the training and the racing. I'm sick of cycling.

The morning after the phone call with Boogerd, I call my father. "Dad, I'm quitting." It's quiet for a moment. Then he says, "Okay, son."

I can hear the relief in his voice.

33

A TURN OF THE TABLES

EMPTINESS. THE DAYS STRETCH OUT BEFORE ME like the ocean from a desert island. I have nothing to do. No need to train, no need to worry about an upcoming race or where the next contract is coming from. Nothing needs doing. And so nothing's exactly what I do. The days immediately after my retirement are largely spent in bed, thinking. There's plenty of time for that now that my life is at a standstill. I blame myself for a lot of things. The fact that my cycling career is over at the age of 30 is mostly my own fault. I've failed. I've squandered my potential.

After a week of solitary confinement at home, Nathalie tells me to come to Los Angeles. I'm on a plane the next day. It's a one-way ticket. Nathalie opens her door to a boy of 30 who has no idea what to do with his life. And she takes him in. She's not all that impressed by my problems. I spend week after week with her. She is a blessing, everything I need. We talk deep into the night. We do things I've never done before. We go to art fairs and museums, attend parties with people I've only ever seen in Hollywood blockbusters. I don't know what I would have done without Nathalie. Life after cycling could have been very different. I could have tumbled into that bottomless pit again, fueled by all the alcohol I could consume. Happiness would have been so far out of reach, God knows where I would have ended up.

In the States, the world of cycling is a long way off, both literally and figuratively. The distance does wonders, helps me put things in perspective. I see that I've been running in circles all these years, a dog chasing his own tail. Whether it's cycling or women or drink, it's the same old routine. I'm always craving more, and for that very reason I usually come up empty-handed. If you're never satisfied, never have patience, want everything all at once, try to cram a hundred different lives into a single lifetime, how can you ever be happy with what you've got? For years I've chased after every temptation that crossed my path without ever stopping to think of the consequences. I've run myself ragged. Swung a wrecking ball at my own career. Caused endless pain to the people around me.

At times I catch myself looking at someone else in the mirror, a man from another time, another life. It's as if I have left the past behind me.

Until the phone rings. It's another call from Switzerland.

It's the past calling. At the other end of the line is a UCI lawyer, Simon Geinoz. He tells me he's building a disciplinary case against Michael Boogerd. It's a thorn in his side that a doping offender is starting his own team with a whole pack of young riders under his guidance. The UCI is gathering evidence against Boogerd with a view to securing the longest possible ban—one that doesn't stop at his own doping use but that covers dealing in dope and facilitating doping among other riders. He tells me that he is sending me a document based on my statements to the Dutch Doping Authority. All I have to do is sign it and Michael will be banned for eight years. And, oh yes, if I could be quick about it. They are keen to release the news of his suspension before the official start of the Tour de France in Utrecht. "Good for publicity, you understand. A major Dutch name caught before the start of the Tour in Holland—well, you get the picture."

He hangs up, and I am left dumbstruck.

I spend that night and the nights that follow tossing and turning. What should I do? Should I sign or not? Does Boogerd deserve that ban? And why do they need my signature anyway? I've already told them all they need to know. More to the point, why place the responsibility for an eight-year ban on my shoulders? Why should I be the one who decides the fate of Michael Boogerd?

I try to put the phone call out of my mind, but I don't have a hope: Geinoz e-mails me and calls again. He piles on the pressure. He wants that signed document back as soon as possible. I talk it over with Nathalie, and with Martijn and Eelco. But in the end they all say the same thing: The decision on whether to sign is up to me. I consider calling Michael personally but eventually decide against it. Not least because I still haven't worked out what to do.

The one thing I'm not about to do is sign before the Tour de France gets under way in Utrecht. I think it's absurd that the UCI wants to hang Boogerd out to dry just as Dutch cycling steps into the spotlight to host the start of the biggest event on the racing calendar. I'm not going to be party to some twisted publicity stunt. If the UCI is that desperate to dress up its image, it can find some other way. This sudden urgency is farcical. It's been over two years since Boogerd made his doping confession. If the UCI has let it rest all this time, one month sooner or later isn't going to make much difference. Not that Geinoz sees it that way. He sends me an e-mail threatening to come after me for refusing to cooperate and reminds me that another suspension could still be in the cards. I laugh out loud when I read that. If they want to slap a cycling ban on a guy who's no longer a cyclist, let them do their worst.

Even so, the whole situation has me feeling uneasy. In July 2015 I travel to France for a commercial project with an insurance firm. I'm accompanying a group of older cyclists who are riding the Tour de France route on tandems. We ride over the cols of the Tour, and the newspapers are full of cycling. I see the peloton on every TV screen—all I have to do is narrow my eyes and I'm right there in the thick of it. That's where I belong, in among that leading group. Suddenly cycling is up close and personal again, and it hurts more than I thought it would. All day I ride or watch other men cycling, in the evenings I drink more than is good for me, and at night I dream of the UCI and its documents.

On July 15, I am a guest on a late-night Dutch chat show, *Tour du Jour*, which looks back at the action from that day's stage of the Tour. One of the other guests is Michael Boogerd. Live on TV, he and presenter Wilfred Genee stitch me up, making me out to be little better than a stool pigeon. For minutes on end all they bang on about is what I told the Doping Authority. It's Michael playing the victim again. I have to remind them that there's only one person at the table who has actually served a doping ban, and that's yours truly.

Even when the cameras stop rolling, Michael won't let it go. He complains about all the money he's had to shell out in lawyers' fees and that he's afraid the UCI is going to ban him. How is he supposed to live without cycling? To my surprise, he even brings up the decision not to give me a contract with Roompot. "Suppose I had given you a contract and next week they slap a ban on me— what good would that have done me?" I frown at him. He says the same thing again. I can feel my blood start to simmer. He decided not to give me a contract because it would have done him no good? It's all I can do not to explode. I snap at him that if our roles had been reversed, I'd have given him a contract if I'd had to explain away his wooden leg.

After my encounter with Michael I spend a couple of days toying with the idea of signing that UCI document. It's revenge, nothing more, nothing less. If he is only thinking of himself, why shouldn't

I do the same? It will destroy him; he is counting on a two-year ban at most. Yet there's plenty to be said for an eight-year suspension. He used dope himself, he taught me how to use it, he sold me Dynepo, and he gave me Matschiner's number. If Michael had been a Kazakh and not the blond, blue-eyed boy of Dutch cycling, no one would have shed a tear if he'd been banned for life. I know it would finish him, eight years in the wilderness. One squiggle on a dotted line from me, and his world comes tumbling down.

I don't sign. Of course I don't. The UCI can stick its statement where the sun don't shine. I've already said my piece for the Doping Authority, been to see WADA, told my story to the press—there's evidence enough if they want to act on it. My signature might put the UCI in a stronger legal position against Boogerd, but if he was that important to the UCI, it should have shot him down earlier. Besides, I don't want to be the one to hand over Michael's head on a platter. I don't want the weight of that eight-year ban on my shoulders.

One reason stands out above all the others: I'm not about to have Michael strung up for something that was my own doing. Michael didn't force dope on me; I went looking for it myself. All kinds of people have played a part in my doping history, but ultimately there can be no doubt about the main culprit: It was me, no one else. Sure, I can get angry about the way things have gone, about the system that molded me. But taking that anger out on other people is another matter.

I let the UCI know that I'm not going to sign its statement. It bans Michael Boogerd for two years—only for his own doping use, not for helping others. A few weeks after my decision not to sign, I receive a contrite e-mail from Simon Geinoz. He writes that he went too far in threatening to ban me and concedes that his tone was far from appropriate. He goes on to convey the UCI's sincere thanks for my commendable assistance in the fight for clean athletes. I read his e-mail with a mixture of satisfaction and amazement.

Apologies and a thank you from the UCI. I never thought I'd see the day.

34

THE STORY OF MY DESCENT

MY LIFE COULD HAVE PANNED OUT ANY NUMBER OF WAYS. I could have wound up in the gutter. I could have avoided exposure as a doping cheat and—with two Liège–Bastogne–Liège titles, an Amstel Gold Race, and a handful of Tour stages to my name—be gearing up for a new season as a leading rider in some team or other. I could just as easily be dead.

I'm not proud of my cycling career. Nor am I proud of the choices I've made over the past 10 years. As a 20-year-old rider, wet behind the ears, I could never have imagined going on to live the life that has filled the pages of this book. I thought I would win major races and carve my name in the annals of cycling in big, bold letters. That didn't happen. I gave in to every temptation that crossed my path. Whether it was money, sex, or booze, my appetite knew no bounds. I was too young, too immature, too impatient, too self-destructive, too cocky to see that I was heading straight for a cliff edge. At times I flew, but I have fallen so much deeper. And after the fall, I spent years sprawled on the ground, unable to pick myself up again. I have fought an endless battle with myself, a battle I lost more often than not. It somehow never dawned on me that my past would define my future to the extent that it has.

I have plenty of regrets. About what I put myself through and, more important, what I put others through. At times I've been a lousy friend, a dick of a teammate, a worthless son. My mother still feels her stomach knot every time my name flashes up on her phone, scared that I've got myself into yet another scrape. For months, even years, I banished my parents, my friends, and my girlfriend to the outer edges of my life, often when I needed them most. But lately things have been better than they were. I've finally shaken off the role of the invincible tough guy who's out to deny responsibility for his own actions.

It's only in recent years that I've been able to see my actions for what they were, take stock of the damage I've done. I have made a mess of things. The aim of this book is to clear up part of that mess. Call it a confession, a bid to free myself from the ugly truth that's been festering inside me for years. I don't need people to like me. I'm not seeking their approval, their pity. My one aim is to talk about where it all went wrong, if only as a warning to the budding Thomas Dekkers of this world. I hope that young athletes can avoid the mistakes I made. I hope that they, and the people guiding them, see the pitfalls along the way before it's too late. And I hope that cycling will change. The sport is no longer swamped with dope the way it was when I was starting out, but it's still far from clean. It's still a world that's riddled with shady agents, untrustworthy team managers, dishonest doctors, and riders with a talent for fooling themselves and everyone around them. And if no one talks about these things, that's how it will always be.

There are times when I miss cycling. It can hurt to see riders my own age stepping onto the podium of a grand tour. I miss the blood, the sweat, the camaraderie in the peloton, the adrenaline of the battle to be first across that finish line. At times I miss having an all-consuming sense of purpose in life. But far more often there's a feeling of relief at no longer being a cyclist. In hindsight, I'm glad I didn't get that contract with Roompot; I would only have ended up fighting my own demons all over again. And Michael Boogerd and Erik Breukink into the bargain.

By and large, I'm happier since I quit. Living in a world outside the peloton is helping me shake off the shadows of the past. I've sold my apartment in Lucca, and my house in Lommel is up for sale. I spend a lot of time traveling with Nathalie. I talk to people who know nothing about cycling and more about the essential things in life. I still go to extremes from time to time. I played a bit part in a film about Lance Armstrong, a death scene that ended up on the cutting-room floor. I took part in *Expedition Robinson*, a survival reality TV show, braving weeks of endless rain on an island with next to no food. The day after I left the show, I was bobbing around in a Greek swimming pool knocking back the finest Champagne.

The difference now is that I can see the extremes for what they are. I ended up cutting short that trip to Greece because it all got to be too much for me. Not that I'm a saint or light-years removed from the bouts of stupidity that got me here in the first place. My character hasn't changed; I still have that hunger for more and the tendency to throw myself over the edge in pursuit of all the temptations that come my way. But now—perhaps for the first time in my life—I am able to put on the brakes. I'm still locked in a battle, but it's starting to feel more like I'm winning.

As for what I want to do with my life . . . fucked if I know. I'm still searching. Art fairs and jet-set parties are fun and even fulfilling in their way, but ultimately it's not the kind of fulfillment that can sustain me. I'll find something. I'm in no hurry, not anymore. First I'm taking the time to clear my head of the debris of the past 10 years.

In the spring of 2016, I'm asked to be part of a theater show. It's called *Sport Monologues*: Six very different athletes take to the stage one by one and tell their stories. The idea is that I'm up there on my own for 20 minutes, telling an audience how I killed off my own cycling career. I agree to do it. In the weeks before opening night, anxiety starts to take hold. I wonder if I'll be able to do this, if I have the guts, if I'll remember my lines, and most of all, if I'll be able to stand there with a couple of thousand people staring back at me and show my weaknesses. Ten years earlier I was lying in a darkened hotel room watching as my blood filled a bag supplied by Eufemiano Fuentes. In the theater I'll be out there on my own, describing that moment with all eyes fixed on me.

That night in September, I wait in the wings of Amsterdam's Kleine Komedie theater. Dressed in my cycling kit, I pace up and down in the shadows backstage, listening to the words spoken by the athletes who are on before me. I hear the audience applaud, feel the heat of the stage lights. I'm so nervous I throw up. I repeat my opening lines over and over in my head. I think of the shitstorm of secrets that I'm about to unleash on the audience. My name is called. There's no way back.

I take a deep breath and step into a thousand colors of light.

EPILOGUE

I first interviewed Thomas Dekker in August 2008. Until that point, I only knew him from the stories I had heard: He was arrogant, suffered from delusions of grandeur, and had way too much money for such a young upstart. At our first meeting, Thomas went out of his way to live up to every one of those preconceptions. I flew out to Pisa, and he picked me up from the airport in his Porsche. As he was stuffing my backpack into the minuscule trunk, he pointed at his gray jogging pants. "Hundred percent cashmere," he bragged, and proceeded to drop the price into the conversation as casually as possible: "Six hundred euros, give or take." I think he was out to impress, but it was more comical than anything. Six hundred euros for a pair of gray jogging pants—it gave me a chuckle all the way from Pisa to his apartment in Lucca. In the days that followed, the arrogant, deluded Thomas Dekker quickly faded into the background, to be replaced by an insecure young man a long way from home, a lad hiding behind a carefree tough-guy façade.

One year later I was back in Lucca. Thomas was still working hard to shore up that façade, even though the UCI had just exposed him as a doping cheat. He acted as if he had everything under control, as if he would sit out his two-year ban and bounce back stronger than ever. He told me he had only ever used dope once. I told him I didn't believe him. He shrugged his shoulders and laughed. "Okay then, don't."

His doping confession came in fits and starts. His transition from the old ways of cycling to the new ways of cycling was like a supertanker changing course, so slow it was sometimes hard to tell what his position was. It was a process that ultimately took years, and it was not until November 2012 that the façade finally crumbled. The US Anti-Doping Agency had just published its report, Rabobank had withdrawn its sponsorship from the cycling team, the world of cycling was in meltdown—yet again—and Thomas had grown sick of it all.

He wanted to shake off the past. He wanted to take a hard look at himself in the mirror, and he hoped that the world of cycling was prepared to do the same. At an office in Amsterdam he told me the story of his doping past. It took him four hours. His testimony formed the basis for a series of articles that were published in the Dutch daily *NRC Handelsblad*, articles about doping within the Rabobank team, the riders who were serviced by Eufemiano

Fuentes, and the abuse of the therapeutic exemption system to enable cortisone injections. We also spoke for the first time about the prospect of writing a book. For both of us there was one condition: If we tell this story, we tell all. No hidden agendas, no excuses, no smoothing away the rough edges—the truth and nothing but the truth, warts and all.

The prospect became a plan, and the plan became a project. We sat across the table from one another countless times, hour after hour, day after day. Thomas talked, I asked questions. He described most of the situations in great detail—even those of which he was most ashamed. He looked back on his life with brutal honesty; over the course of our conversations he never tried to spare himself, never sought to gloss over his behavior or the choices he had made.

This is Thomas Dekker's story, the events of his life as seen through his eyes. However, that is not to say that Thomas's first-hand accounts are the only source. This book is also the result of many hours of research. Over the past few years I have spoken to as many of the people who feature in these pages as possible, and I have verified Thomas's version of events against court records and the police files of Operation Puerto.

Not everyone who is part of this story was prepared to cooper-ate. Some did not respond to my attempts to contact them, some refused to comment, and a number of doctors declined on the grounds of patient confidentiality. Others repudiated Thomas's version of events then and still do. His former manager Jacques Hanegraaf denies having put Thomas in touch with Eufemiano

Fuentes and disputed the truth of the book in a open court hearing. His case was heard, and his claims were rejected. Michael Boogerd does not feel that he has been accurately portrayed in all of the situations described by Thomas. Belgian doctor Jan Mathieu says that he did not invent injuries in order to obtain therapeutic-use exemptions. Daan Luijkx strenuously denies knowing anything about the relationship between Thomas Dekker and Eufemiano Fuentes. With the corroboration of his business partner Hoendervangers, he also denies having said the words "Okay, and if not we'll figure something out together."

This book in no way resembles the book that Thomas had in mind when we first spoke to each other in 2008. He wanted to tell an uplifting story packed with euphoric tales of victory and sporting glory. Instead, it became the story of his descent into doping and disillusionment, an account of his battle with himself. For years he has been his own worst enemy. Sometimes he still is. But the biggest difference between Thomas then and Thomas now is that he is no longer pretending to be somebody he's not. He has dropped the pose of the invincible superman.

The last time I saw him, he was wearing gray jogging pants. "Cashmere?" I asked. He shook his head. "Nah, H&M. Fifteen ninety-five."

He laughed even louder than I did.

—THIJS ZONNEVELD

ABOUT THE COAUTHOR

Thijs Zonneveld is a Dutch sports journalist and a former professional cyclist. He covers the sport of cycling for Rotterdam's leading newspaper, *AD Algemeen Dagblad*. He also delivers commentary for Dutch public television. In 2016, he received the award for Best Dutch Sports Journalist for *Descent*.